# Introduction To Precious Metal Clay

## A Do-It-Yourself Master Class

by Mary Ann Devos

# Wardell

## PUBLICATIONS INC

- Printed in Thailand by Phongwarin Printing Ltd.
- Published simultaneously in Canada and USA
- Distributed worldwide, inquire for dealer list
- Email: info@wardellpublications.com
- Website: www.wardellpublications.com

## Acknowledgements from the Author

- The inspiration and support for this book have come from many sources. I have learned so much from watching my students approach this magical clay material. Sharing the process with you has helped me to further develop these techniques. I wish I could list all of you.

- A special thanks goes to Tim McCreight, Consultant for Mitsubishi Materials Corporation, my first PMC teacher.

- I wish to express my gratitude to Earl Roberts, manager of PMC Connection and president of Sierra Thermal Industries, Inc., manufacturer of Sierra kilns. He is a great business partner and has encouraged me since the beginning of my silver clay career. I am proud to be the Director of Education for PMC Connection and to work with such a progressive, innovative team.

- Thanks to Mr. Masao Hoshide, President of Mikuni American, Inc. for his support of PMC Connection.

- Thanks to Mr. Dennis Nakashima, Vice President of Mikuni American, Inc. for all his kindness and guidance.

- I wish to thank Mr. Akira Nishio, Vice General Manager, and Mr. Atsushi Nishiyama, Assistant Manager of the Advanced Products Company of Mitsubishi Materials Corporation of Japan. They have been very generous and encouraging.

- I thank Mr. Eisuke Kojima and Mr. Daisuke Kojima, of SunArt, for helping to facilitate our bi-cultural connection.

- All of the Senior Teachers of the PMC Connection are a joy to share this experience with. They are a dynamic teaching team. Thanks to Linda Bernstein, Sondra Busch, Mary Ellin D'Agostino, Sherry Fotopoulos, Vera Lightstone and Marlynda Taylor.

- A book like this would not be possible without the wonderful photography and editing skills of my publisher Randy Wardell.

- Ken Devos, my husband, has provided a tremendous amount of support for all my traveling, teaching and book writing. He offers computer, editorial, photographic and emotional support to all our endeavors and I appreciate him greatly.

### Cataloging in Publication Data

Devos, MaryAnn

Introduction to precious metal clay / author: MaryAnn Devos ; senior editor: Ken Devos ;

Includes index.

ISBN 0-919985-36-X

1. Precious metal clay. I. Devos, Ken II. Wardell, Randy A. (Randy Allan), 1954- III. Title.

TT213.D49 2002        739.2        C2002-902238-X

# Introduction to Precious Metal Clay

**Author & Designer**
MaryAnn Devos

**Senior Editor**
Ken Devos

**Text Editor**
Randy Wardell

**Jewelry Design & Fabrication**
MaryAnn Devos

**Photography**
Randy Wardell, Rob Stegmann and
Ken Devos (except as noted on photos)

**Digital Photo Retouching**
Bill Reshetar

**Book Layout & Typography**
Randy Wardell and Barbara Bert Silbert

**Cover Design**
Christine Arleij

**Dedication**
This book is dedicated to our grandchildren: Kyle, Cierra, Braden, & Tristan

**Publisher**
Randy Wardell

Published by

# Wardell
## PUBLICATIONS INC

To receive our electronic newsletter or to send suggestions please contact us
by Email: info@wardellpublications.com or visit our website: www.wardellpublications.com

# A Message from the Author

Precious Metal Clay (referred to as 'PMC' throughout this book) is one of the most remarkable developments in metal working since lost wax casting was developed thousands of years ago. This product is manufactured by Mitsubishi Materials Corporation and is available in fine silver (0.999%) and 22K gold. It is composed of microscopic metal particles, a non-toxic organic binder and water. It looks, feels and is shaped just like potter's clay but after firing all that is left is solid precious metal.

My love for this material began in late 1996 when I purchased with my first lump of PMC. In January of 1997 I took a technique class conducted by Tim McCreight, who is a metals instructor, author and consultant to Mitsubishi Materials Corp. Soon after that class was completed silver clay became my full-time endeavor. I distributed my work through art galleries, museum shops and juried art shows. I also began teaching in 1997 and to this day my greatest joy comes from coaching, sharing and developing new PMC techniques. It has been my privilege to train under a master teacher in Japan and in turn I have taught silver clay techniques all over the United States, Canada, Europe, and also in Japan.

The process requires much less equipment and training than traditional metal work, making it easily accessible to artists, hobby-crafters, fine jewelers and metal-smiths. The material is so 'user friendly' that people of any age or creative background can be instantly successful.

My own education continues on a daily basis as I explore along with my students as we push the boundaries. PMC can be combined with many materials such as semi-precious gems, glass, porcelain, ceramics, sculpture, and mixed metals, among others. Every successful artist develops a unique personal style. What is so provocative about this new material is that we are developing and sharing innovative techniques as we draw from our own artistic or technical backgrounds. The fact is we are participating in the groundbreaking creation of a new standard.

My personal work is greatly influenced by nature and ancient art and I have always been attracted to organic, textural and primitive designs. I find it intriguing to echo the nature of PMC's clay-like beginning. Born of clay and fire, it is transformed into a precious metal work.

This book will guide you all the way through the basic forming techniques but you will soon learn that you are limited only by your imagination. So have fun, be creative and live the process, become one with the clay and join us as pioneers in this new medium.

MaryAnn Devos

PS: Remember - Safety first! See list on page 96

Kabookie Dancer - using Dichroic glass & a porcelain mask
*Photo by: Randy Wardell*

**Author Contact Information:**

PMC Connection
303 Donora Blvd,
Fort Myers Beach, FL 33931
Phone: 239-463-8006
Email: pmcconnection@aol.com
Website: www.pmcconnection.com

# TABLE OF CONTENTS

## THE PROJECTS

## SUPPLEMENTARY MATERIAL

# What Is PMC? History and Uses

For thousands of years humans have manipulated precious metals to create and enhance personal adornments. Jewelry has always been an important means of self-expression. Gold and silver began as primitive fabricated ornaments. The use of heat in the metalworking process led to various casting methods. Over time metal working techniques have advanced with the improvements of equipment but the basics have remained essentially the same.

The development of Precious Metal Clay (PMC) by Mitsubishi Materials Corporation in the early 1990's created a unique material for use in jewelry making. The company was looking for innovative and profitable ways to use their mined and recycled precious metals. Their scientists developed PMC and have obtained several patents for its use.

Precious Metal Clay is composed of precious metal particles (fine silver, gold or platinum), a non-toxic organic binder and water. The metal particles are measured in microns. The proportions of metal, binder and water vary depending upon the type of the material: clay, syringe or paste. Each has progressively more water. In each instance there is just enough binder present to hold the metal together in a workable, clay-like form.

PMC Standard must be fired in a kiln to sinter or fuse the metal powder. This process also drives off any remaining water and burns off the organic binder. This sintering requires a temperature of 1650°F (800°C) for a period of 2 hours. The result is solid metal with the characteristics similar to those of cast precious metal.

Shortly after the introduction of PMC into the United States, Mitsubishi modified the metal component of the material, using particles even smaller than those used in PMC Standard.

A 26 gram package of PMC Standard clay in 'lump-type' form.

With the metal particle size reduced, the new clay form, called PMC+, was even denser than the original. The clay contained a greater percentage of metal and smaller percentages of binder and water. This resulted in two major changes. The shrinkage that comes from the drying and sintering process was decreased from 30 percent to 12 percent. Also, the firing time was reduced from 2 hours to only 10 minutes.

Further work with the new material found even greater flexibility in the sintering process. In addition to the 10 minute firing at 1650°F (900°C), it is possible to fire the material at a lower temperature while increasing the firing time to allow for complete sintering. It is possible to fire PMC+ at 1560°F (850°C) for 20 minutes or at 1470°F (800°C) for 30 minutes. This innovation makes it possible to incorporate materials that have a lower firing temperature (such as glass & some gemstones) into the pieces prior to the firing process.

Research continues in the development of PMC products. New forms, such as the Sheet type and PMC3 have recently been introduced and artists eager to incorporate them into the creation of their unique jewelry pieces. Sheet type eliminates the water component of the clay, increasing the working time tremendously. PMC3, with metal particle size even smaller than those in PMC+, enables an even lower firing temperature.

With each new product, artists become aware of more applications of the material to their creative processes and researchers recognize further modifications that will facilitate this process. The end result is a wealth of materials and techniques that are available to artists regardless of their degree of technical expertise.

NOTE: Unless otherwise stated, the silver clay material used in the projects throughout this book was PMC+, although PMC3 could have been used since the shrinkage factor is the same.

'Tribal Mask' featuring Cubic Zirconia gemstone eyes.
*Photo by: Randy Wardell*

## SILVER CLAY

• **PMC Standard Clay:** This product is available in the 'lump-clay' material format only and is also the most economical of all the PMC materials (see photo on previous page). PMC Standard lump-clay can be rolled into sheets, pinch formed, 'snake' coiled among other methods to make a great variety of personal adornments. This PMC 'Standard' material shrinks in volume about 30% from the wet or moldable stage to the finished fired stage. This shrinkage must be taken into account when designing your piece but can be considered an advantage when you are working on a highly detailed piece as the shrinking actually intensifies the surface texture and details. As a result it is better to use PMC+ or PMC3 for rings or other items that must be a specific size when completed.

Due to the combination of high firing temperature and long firing times we do not recommend using PMC Standard with fused glass. However lab grown stones fire well with this clay form.

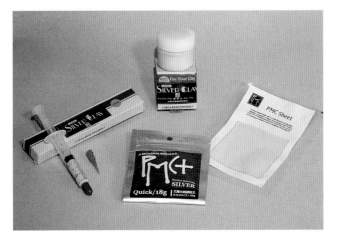

PMC clay showing the 4 forms that are available. Clockwise from top: Paste type, Sheet Type, Lump Type, Syringe type.

• **PMC+:** The chief advantage is this clay product (as compared to PMC Standard) is that it only shrinks about 12% from the wet or moldable stage to the finished fired stage. This means that the piece you're working on will be almost the same size when finish-fired, as it was when you were working on it. Also because the shrinkage is smaller and measurable, you can make rings and other items that must have a more precise size (you will learn how to allow for shrinkage in a ring project on page 20).

## TYPES OF PMC

PMC Standard, PMC+, PMC3 and PMC Gold are composed of powdered precious metals, (fine silver or 22K gold), a non-toxic organic binder (the clay substrate) and water. The primary differences among the three materials are the firing times, firing temperatures and shrinkage rates. Each of these factors is a result of the differences in the metal particle sizes and the percentages of binder in the clay. The following chart compares the firing information for all four types in both silver and 22K gold.

| Product Type | Firing Temperature | Firing Time | Shrinkage |
|---|---|---|---|
| PMC Standard | 1650°F / 900°C | 2 hours | 30% |
| PMC+ | 1650°F / 900°C | 10 minutes | 12% |
| PMC+ | 1560°F / 850°C | 20 minutes | 12% |
| PMC+ | 1470°F / 800°C | 30 minutes | 12% |
| PMC3 | 1290°F / 700°C | 10 minutes | 12% |
| PMC3 | 1110°F / 600°C | 45 minutes | 12% |
| PMC 22K Gold | 1650°F / 900°C | 10 minutes | 14% |

PMC+ is available in several material forms (listed below) that effectively increase the workability of this most versatile product.

• **PMC+ Lump Clay:** This is the lump-clay form of this

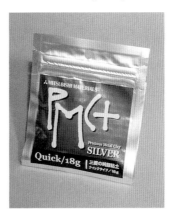

particular product. It is excellent for making items that will incorporate stone settings or fused glass cabochons (due to the low shrinkage rate). It is easy to shape with your fingers by rolling, coiling or sculpting into a great variety of shapes.

• **PMC3 Syringe:** This product comes already loaded into a syringe-type applicator. It can be used alone or in combination with any of the other PMC material forms. Use it to create filigree type designs or fanciful rings. We often use it to embellish our lump-clay or paste work and it makes a great way to form those stone settings. We also use it to decorate porcelain, hand built pottery, contemporary ceramics or

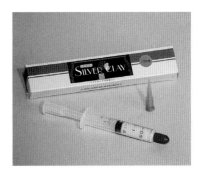

porcelain dolls.

- **PMC+ Paste:** This product comes in a small jar and is the consistency of white glue. It is normally applied to your work with a small artist's paintbrush. This material format is used as a glue to help assemble your lump-clay pieces. It can fill

and smooth edges and joints and will fill any cracks or blemishes in your piece after it has dried (but before firing). The paste format also enables us to make 'hollow-form' items by painting the material directly onto the surface of a burnable core. It can be applied to natural leaves, paper forms (e.g. origami) or many other organic materials to create a perfect, fine silver impression of the original item.

- **PMC+ Sheet:** This product is a thin, square sheet approximately 2-1/4" square (5.7 cm). This material format contains no water. This means it does not dry out or crack. It feels like a piece of vinyl and is well suited for origami constructions or for simulating fabric or other silver sheet-metal applications.

'Bad Hair Day' Hand formed mask inset with fine silver wire and wrapped with 26 gauge gold wire and gold beads.

*Photo by: Steve Meltzer*

- **PMC3:** This is the most recent product in the PMC line-up and is available in lump, syringe, and paste form. It has the same basic working characteristics as PMC+ but fires at a lower temperature range of 1290°F / 700°C for 10 minutes or 1110°F / 600°C for 45 minutes.

## GOLD CLAY 22K

- **PMC Gold Clay 22K:** is available in "lump-clay" form only. It shrinks about 14% (slightly more than PMC+ or PMC3). The firing temperature is between 1650°F /900°C with a firing time of 10 minutes to a low of 1290°F / 700°C for 90 minutes. It is possible to make a paste from the lump gold clay to fill cracks & joints. Just add a little water and mix. PMC Gold models and takes textures just like silver clay. It is possible to use both gold and silver PMC in the same project by firing the piece at the appropriate silver temperature for the required gold firing time.

'Tribal Mask 2' made using PMC Standard and features lab grown stone (in forehead) glass beads and an unusual pearl.

*Photo by: Ken Devos*

This photo shows the elegantly understated packaging for PMC's 22K gold clay, available in lump form only.

# THE BASICS

Store PMC in a cool, dry location. Store all unused portions in the original foil package with a few drops of water; be sure to completely seal the package after squeezing out the air.

If the clay begins to dry as you work with it, use a moist paintbrush to apply water to the surface of the clay. Allow the water to sink into the clay before proceeding (a few seconds is all it takes).

Tools for working with the clay are straightforward and uncomplicated. We use potter's clay shapers, cutters and texture tools, plus leather working tools, craft knives and other assorted objects normally found around the home or shop (see pages 14-19 for tools and equipment).

When assembling PMC Standard we use a paste, made from a small amount of clay mixed with water, to secure the joints. For best results when working with PMC+ or PMC3 use the paste clay made specifically for that product type.

Dry your work well before firing. The clay will air dry if left out overnight. You can speed up the process using a hair dryer, an electric griddle or a toaster oven set at about 150 to 200°F (80 to 92°C). You can use the hair dryer either hand-held or as part of a drying box. (See page 20)

Use the firing schedule for the most sensitive material being used, e.g. when firing a piece that contains glass use the temperature and time settings for glass, which is more sensitive than the silver. Be sure to refer to the specific firing instructions outlined in addendum 1 on page 80.

PMC is well suited for carving in the leather hard or bone-dry state. You can shape it with carving tools, chisels, files, scrapers, Dremel™ and other similar tools.

'Victorian Garden' featuring Silver clay (lump, paste & syringe) plus natural pearls, fine silver wire, and a large lab grown gemstone. *Photo by: Randy Wardell*

Finishing should be completed as much as possible in the 'bone-dry' or unfired clay state. It is much easier to file or sand clay than solid metal. When it is bone dry you can sand and smooth it easily using emery boards or sandpaper. You can even use an alcohol free wet wipe to smooth the surfaces. Spending time to finish your piece in this state will improve your results tremendously.

Fired silver will have a white surface. This is the way all fine silver looks after firing because the surface is rough. Light is not reflected well from this bumpy surface, resulting in a dull appearance. You will need to smooth it with a stainless steel wire brush. This will give the silver a matt finish. You can obtain a high shine finish by using a burnishing tool or a rotary tumbler (see finishing on page 86).

PMC is fine (pure) silver, with no other metals included. It is softer than alloyed silvers such as sterling. Sterling is a combination of silver (92.5%) and copper (7.5%). The addition of copper makes sterling stronger than fine silver. Therefore, chain links, bails or clasps made from fine silver should be thicker than those made from sterling. Reinforce any thin areas of PMC that may be subject to stress. This is to avoid breakage due to metal fatigue.

The addition of copper in sterling also makes the metal more reactive to heat and chemicals. Sterling will react during firing to form a 'fire-scale' that is a blackening of the metal surface caused by the oxidation of the copper content. This scale can be removed using jeweler's pickle solution. This firing process also can result in a weakening of the sterling, making the metal more brittle and subject to breakage. If you insert and fire sterling silver, use wire 16 gauge or larger to maintain strength. Also it is better to use PMC3, with its lower firing temperature, if you plan to incorporate Sterling silver components.

'Fish Tale' Hand sculptured fish pendant with sterling wire chain and glass beads. *Photo by: Ken Devos*

# GLOSSARY

Due to the clay-like nature of PMC, many of the terms used in this book are taken from the world of pottery as well as those used by gold and silversmiths. Listed below is a glossary of terms we use frequently.

## A

**Alloy:** a metal that combines two or more component metals, usually to create a metal with one or more characteristics not found in the individual metals. For example, sterling is an alloy of silver (92.5%) and copper (7.5%) that is harder than either silver or copper individually.

**Antiquing:** see Patina, also Pickle Solution

## B

**Bail:** a metal loop that attaches to a pendant, through which you pass a chain or cord.

**Bezel pusher:** a polished steel hand tool that is used to set a stone in a bezel mount. It consists of a small wooden handle and a steel shaft, which is used to push or bend the bezel wire next to the stone, which has been placed inside the bezel.

**Bezel setting:** a stone mount, usually for cabochons, in which a strip of metal attached to a base encircles the stone and holds it in place. Usually you create a circle or oval (bezel) sized to the stone to be attached and fuse it to the metal base. Place the stone into the bezel and use a bezel pusher (see above) to move the bezel against the stone. Use a burnishing tool to smooth the bezel and place it as close to the stone as possible, insuring a tight fit.

**Bezel wire:** a thin metal strip, available in different widths, and used to encircle a gemstone to attach the stone to a metal base.

This simple elegant silver clay pendant and matching clasp is further enhanced by the natural amethyst and silver bead necklace chain. *Photo by: Randy Wardell*

**Bone dry:** the condition of the clay after it is completely dried but before it is fired. In this state it is possible to carve the clay using files, cutters and scrapers.

**Burnished:** the highly polished state of the fired silver after it is worked with either a burnishing tool or tumbled in a rotary tumbler with stainless steel shot. Also known as mirror finish.

## C

**Cabochon:** A glass gem or bead, semi precious stone, or lab grown stone cut in convex form, and usually highly polished but not faceted.

**Casting grain:** small pellets of metal such as fine silver, brass, or gold. The metal is melted and poured into molds to create new pieces. They are used with PMC as decorative elements.

**Ceramic fiber blanket:** a special lightweight insulation material designed for use in high temperature kilns. It usually is in a form similar to cotton wool and available in sheets of varying thickness.

**Ceramic fiber kiln shelf:** a lightweight insulation material designed for use in high temperature kilns. It is available in sheets, usually 1/4" to 1" thick (6 - 25 mm), that is cut to fit inside the kiln as shelving for the PMC pieces when being fired. This material is not susceptible to thermal shock, as is the case with hard ceramic shelves. This feature allows the removal of ceramic fiber shelves from the kiln while the fired pieces are still hot without cracking the shelves.

**Coil or snake:** a thin cylinder or rope of clay that you form by rolling the clay between two flat surfaces. Often these surfaces are a worktable and your hand.

'Fancy Flower' made with hand formed lump clay, fine silver wire and a lab grown ruby crystal. *Photo by: Rob Stegman*

**Cork Clay:** A soft moldable material that is used as a core to create three-dimensional pieces. A cork clay core does not have to be removed from the formed piece before firing because cork clay will 'burn out' in the kiln as the silver clay is firing. All that is left is a bit of ash dust that can be easily removed. (see Project 3 page 29 and Addendum 6 - page 89).

**Cubic Zirconia Stones:** Also called CZ's these lab grown stones are available in many colors. (see Addendum 8 - page 90)

## D, E

**Electric scribe:** an electric vibrating engraver with a tungsten carbide or diamond tip used to sign a name or create a design by hand drawing.

## F

**Fibula:** a clasp resembling a safety pin used especially by the ancient Greeks and Romans. The pin can be created with various design elements using gold or sterling silver wire to complement the pendant that it supports.

**Findings:** A jeweler's term that usually refers to a pre-manufactured component that is added to a jewelry piece. Examples of findings are: earring studs, jump rings, bails, clasps, brooch pins, bezels, etc. Gemstones are not usually described as a finding.

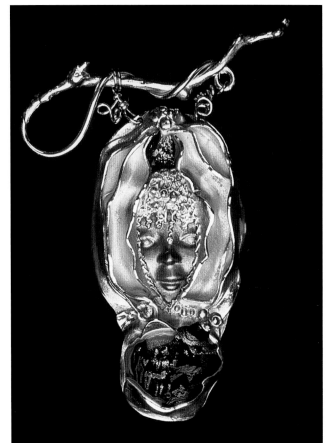

'Spring Peeking Out' This pin uses hand formed lump clay, a silver paste coated twig, 14K gold wire and a miniature ceramic face with a 22K Gold glaze. *Photo by: Rob Stegman*

'Porcelain Serving Utensils' These porcelain utensils were decorated with lump, syringe work and CZ stones.
*Photo by: Ken Devos*

**Fine Silver:** Fine or 'pure' silver means the metal does not have any alloy metals added to it (see Sterling silver). Fine silver is defined as .999 'fineness' and is pure silver (it may contain some natural occurring 'trace' metals)

**Finish, Burnish:** the highly polished state of the fired silver after it is worked with either a burnishing tool or tumbled in a rotary tumbler with stainless steel shot. Also known as mirror finish.

**Finish, Matt:** the state of the fired silver after it has been cleaned and polished using a stainless steel brush. This also is known as a brushed finish.

**Flex-shaft:** a motor driven tool, similar to a Dremel™, but stronger. The motor powers drill bits, grinding stones, sanding disks and polishing wheels attached to a flexible shaft (thus the name).

## G

**Gemstones:** See listings for: Cabochon, Cubic Zirconia, & Lab Grown Stones.

**Girdle (re: gemstone):** the widest part of a faceted gemstone, when you look from the side, also see 'table' in Glossary. (See gemstone setting procedure on page 91 for more details).

**Greenware:** also known as 'bone-dry clay' it is the completely dried condition of the clay before it is fired. This term is borrowed from the ceramics industry.

## H

**High fire kiln release paper:** a commercially available insulation material that is paper thin and used to provide a smooth surface on which to fire glass. It is also used as a separator between a PMC clay item and other solid form-molds used to hold a curve or other shape. Kiln release paper is a one-time use material. After firing the paper becomes powdery. Caution: do not to inhale the dust from fired kiln release paper.

Native Mask - Glass beads and natural feathers are combined in this respectful sculpture. *Photo by: Randy Wardell*

## I, J

**Jump Ring:** a small ring made from wire, usually circular but sometimes oval or other shape. The most common form can be opened at the joint where the two ends of the wire meet. Other types have a soldered joint that cannot be opened. A jump ring is most often used as a mechanical fastener between two or more other objects.

## K, L

**Lab grown gemstone:** a gemstone created in a laboratory setting using the same chemical composition as the natural stone. These stones are pure and usually do not contain 'inclusions', impurities and imperfections found in natural stones. These stones usually will withstand the PMC firing process unaffected.

**Leather hard:** the condition of the clay when mostly dry. In this state it is possible to carve the clay using cutters and scrapers.

## M

**Mallet:** a hammer whose head is made of a resilient material such as rawhide or plastic. This is used to bend and shape metals such as silver without leaving marks.

**MOHS scale:** a measurement that indicates the relative hardness of minerals. It is based upon a ten (10) point scale wherein 1 is the softest material (talc) and 10 is the hardest material (diamond). Note: Do not fire-in natural diamonds. They contain carbon and will be destroyed during the high temperature, long firing schedule.

**Mold making (RTV):** Room Temperature Vulcanization, a process in which a two-part material is mixed to create a mold-making medium. The two parts react chemically to form a stable compound. The process is similar to that of epoxy glue. Before mixing, both parts are soft and malleable. After mixing, the compound remains malleable during the curing process, usually 5-10 minutes. During that time the material can be shaped as a mold. Afterward the mold remains flexible but retains the mold shape.

## N, O, P

**Patina or antiquing:** a process where the silver is colored with various chemical agents. These agents react with the silver to form oxides (a form of tarnish). The nature of the coloring agent (patina), the length of exposure and the concentration of the agent solution determine the resulting color(s). The temperatures of the piece and/or the solution determine the speed of the reaction.

**Parchment Paper:** A semi-transparent paper most often used in cooking for baking or freezing. It is used with silver clay as a forming surface that will easily release the silver clay once it has dried.

'3-D Orchid' This lump clay sculpted silver pendant is featured in project 6 on page 39. *Photo by: Rob Stegman*

**Pickle Solution:** A mix of mild acid usually used warm or hot, to clean the surface of jewelry after firing or soldering metals such as sterling. The solution cleans surface dirt from the jewelry. It also reacts chemically with oxides on the surface created by the heat of the firing or soldering processes. This process is not necessary for fine silver since the firing and soldering processes do not create these oxides.

**Pin back:** the mechanism, like a safety pin, which attaches to the back of a silver piece to allow the wearer to fasten the piece to clothing by passing the sharpened pin through the cloth.

**Prong setting:** a metal mount with three or more upright ends that is used to secure a gemstone to jewelry. One such piece is called the Tiffany setting.

**Pure Silver:** See Fine Silver.

**PVC roller:** Standard PVC plumbing pipe, 1" (2.5 cm) in diameter and cut to 6" (15 cm) long.

## Q, R

**Ring Mandrel:** a mold/form used in the creation of rings. This tapered form is basically a truncated cone, made of wood or metal (see photo on page 15). The wooden mandrel usually is used to form the ring in the wet clay state. The metal mandrel is used to shape the ring after firing, using a rawhide or plastic mallet. In addition there are ceramic mandrels specifically for silver clay forming, that can be fired with the clay to maintain the size and shape of the ring band (see photo on page 20).

**Ring Shank:** the portion of the ring that encircles the finger or toe, often called the band. The shape of the shank, in cross section, determines the type: flat band or round band.

## S

**Shrink lock:** the process whereby PMC+ work is made to fit tightly and securely against another material, such as porcelain. The PMC+ is placed around the other material in an interconnected pattern so that the shrinkage of the silver clay during the firing process will join the materials together permanently.

**Silver:** see Fine Silver, also Sterling Silver

**Slab:** a flat piece of clay, usually created by rolling the clay with a cylindrical tool such as a PVC roller.

**Sterling Silver:** An alloy (see Alloy description) of 92.5% pure silver and 7.5% copper. When these 2 metals are melted together the resulting mixed metal, known as 'Sterling Silver' is actually harder than either the pure silver or copper alone.

**Stake:** a metal form against which to shape metal pieces (see page 93, photo at top center).

'Hearts Entwined' Lump clay textured with rubber stamps plus silver beads and fine silver wire wrap.
*Photo by: Rob Stegman*

## T

**Table (re: gemstone):** the flat top of a faceted gemstone, when looking at the stone from the side, also see 'girdle' in Glossary. (See gemstone setting procedure on page 91 for more details).

**Thickness slats:** These are simply art frame matt board approximately 3/64" (1.2 mm) thick, cut into strips about 1" (2.5 cm) wide by 4" to 6" (10 x 15 cm) long. A an alternative for matt board, stack 3 standard playing cards for each 3/64" (1.2 mm). We use playing cards throughout the book. The advantage is that you can vary the height of the stack, thus the thickness of the clay, in smaller increments than with the matt board.

'Elegant Old Bottle' The silver sculpture was created by coating a gauze bow with paste type clay (the piece was fired separately and added to the glass bottle later).
*Photo by: Rob Stegman*

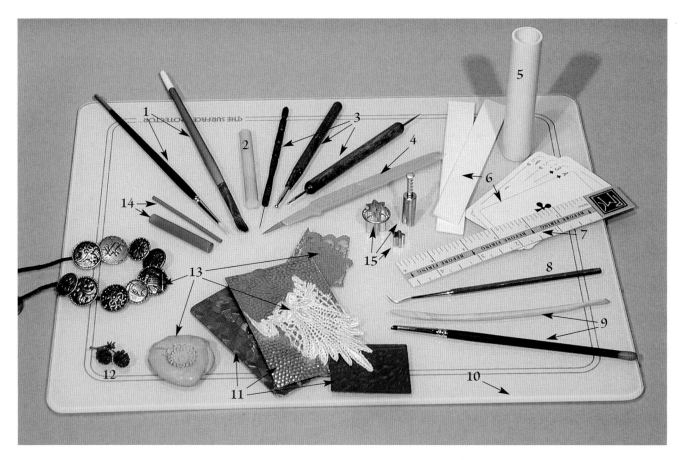

## MODELING TOOLS (photo above):

1. Paintbrushes, artist brushes in assorted sizes
2. Wooden dowels in assorted diameters
3. Clay Tools
4. Craft Knife
5. PVC Roller
6. Thickness Slats (left) or Playing Cards (right)
7. Plastic ruler (with inch & metric numbers)
8. Dental Tools
9. Potter's Clay shaping tools
10. Smooth Work Surface - more details at right
11. Textured Brass Plates
12. Organic Material For Texture and/or Burnout
13. Texture: Lace, Rubber Stamps, Buttons, etc.
14. Drinking And Stirring Straws
15. Clay Shape Cutters, Canapé or Cookie Cutters
16. Plastic Food Wrap (not shown)

## WORKING SURFACES

A smooth working surface that is approximately 12" x 18" (30 cm x 46 cm) is all you will need. PMC is a very clean medium and you will not need a large space on which to work. A smooth working surface is important because it will be much easier to salvage all unused bits and pieces of clay and place them into your clay paste container.

Some good working surfaces are:

• a glass or smooth ceramic kitchen-counter protector (see item 10 above)
• a sheet of standard window glass (with the sharp edges rounded)
• a sheet of Plexiglas
• a smooth plastic placemat
• a 'self-healing' craft cutting mat
• a piece of kitchen-counter laminate
• a plastic page protector

**Tip:** It's always a good idea to lightly coat the working surface with cooking oil, hand balm or similar product, to prevent the clay from sticking to the surface. Be careful to avoid petroleum based lotions or lubricants (eg Vaseline™).

## MISCELLANEOUS (photo below):

1. Molding Compound - details at right
2. White Craft Glue
3. Hand Balm (or cooking oil)
4. Cellophane Adhesive tape
5. Ring Mandrel
6. Ring Sizers
7. Removable adhesive note pads (e.g. Post-it™)
8. Decorative-edged Scissors
9. Scissors (standard)
10. Artist's Palette Knife
11. Carving Tool (used for carving stamp material)
12. Rubber stamp mat material (item at left),
    Linoleum Printing Block (not shown), or
    Polymer Eraser (item at right )
13. Handmade Paper, Origami Paper,
    Drawing Paper
14. Patterned paper punches (hearts, stars etc)
15 Rubber Stamps (not shown)

## MOLD MAKING COMPOUNDS

You can make molds to use with PMC from a variety of materials. Item 1 in the photo below is a 2-part dental mold compound know as RTV (Room Temperature Vulcanization). Almost any mold making material will work such as polymer clay, thermosetting plastics and even silicone based caulking. Just follow the product directions to create the mold. Be sure to apply a light coat of cooking oil (or hand balm) to the inside of the mold before pressing the PMC into the mold.

## RUBBER STAMPS

Rubber stamps are a wonderful source of design and texture for your PMC pieces. However if you choose to make use of this resource you must take notice of the copyright restrictions which some stamp manufacturers place on the use of their stamps. Some manufacturers do not allow any commercial use whatsoever. Thankfully many others allow you to use their designs in the creation of any artwork, for both private and limited commercial purposes. Be sure to read the fine print on the stamps you choose to purchase.

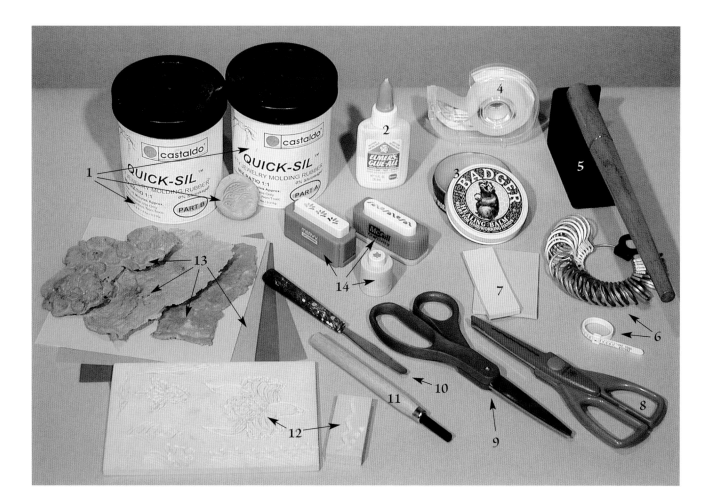

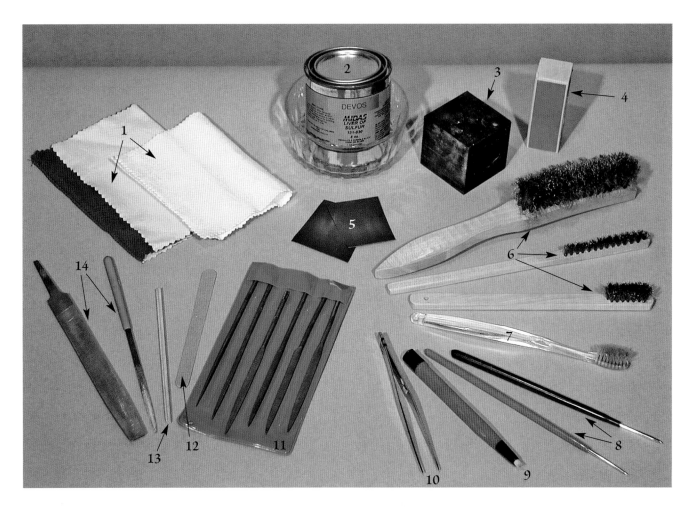

# FINISHING TOOLS (photo above):

1. Rouge Polishing Cloths – removes tarnish for a high gloss finish
2. Liver Of Sulfur – antiquing compound and glass bowl (see addendum 6, pg 87)
3. Hard Rubber Tool Block – used to support jewelry while polishing
4. Buffer block – a soft block with different grit paper on each side
5. Sandpaper or Emerycloth - in 600, 800, 1000 & 1200 grits
6. Wire Brushes: - assorted sizes in stainless steel &/or brass
7. Toothbrush – used for cleaning and buffing
8. Burnishing Tools – the metal end creates a polished, glossy surface
9. Fiberglass Brush – for polishing stones, delicate jewelry and for use on porcelain
10. Tweezers – assorted sizes are useful
11. Needle Files – used for filing & smoothing
12. Emery Board - a.k.a. fingernail files
13. Sanding stick for cleaning ceramic greenware
14. Medium Files – flat, half-round & triangle

Pottery vase decorated with leaf design. 'Fancy Flower' (see photo on page 10 bottom left). *Photo by: Rob Stegman*

## ASSEMBLY TOOLS (photo below):

1. Jeweler's Ball-peen Hammer
2. Plastic (left) or Rawhide (right) Mallet
3. Jeweler's Glue - to secure stones in a bezel
4. Bezel Roller/Setter
5. Metal Ring Mandrel – for holding ring during polishing and texturing
6. Prong Pusher - used to bend prongs while setting stones
7. Tweezers
8. Pin Vise – for hand drilling
9. Magnifying Visor-goggles
10. Jeweler's Loupe
11. Set of Pliers: chain, round, flat nose, side cutter and nylon jaw
12. Dremel™ Tool Bits- grinding and polishing bits
13. Vibrating Scriber Tool (Optional) - used to engrave your artwork with date and name

## ACCESSORIES (Optional) not shown:

- Dremel™ Tool - A small hand-held rotary tool used with bits (see item12) to grind and polish
- Flex Shaft - This power tool is a professional level rotary grinding machine with numerous attachments and multipurpose uses

## EMBELLISHING CERAMIC'S

PMC+ and PMC3 work very well in combination with traditional clay media. Most ceramic clays have a maturation temperature that is higher than PMC material so it is necessary to complete the ceramic object before adding the silver clay embellishments. The degree to which these materials will adhere to each other relies on the porosity of the ceramic clay. If the ceramic clay object is glazed, then the maturation of the glaze will affect the bond of the silver clay embellishment If the glaze softens or "opens up" at the PMC+ or PMC3 firing temperature (1110 °F/600°CR to 1650 °F/700°CR), there will be a more complete and permanent bond than if the glaze does not soften. Frequently glazes for porcelain and other high-fired clays have a maturation temperature much higher than the PMC and there is less bonding between the glaze and the PMC. In these instances we must use a "shrink-lock" technique that takes advantage of the 12% shrinkage of the PMC+ and PMC3. The silver clay embellishment is strategically placed on the ceramic object to form a kind of net that encircles the ceramic piece to securely capture it.

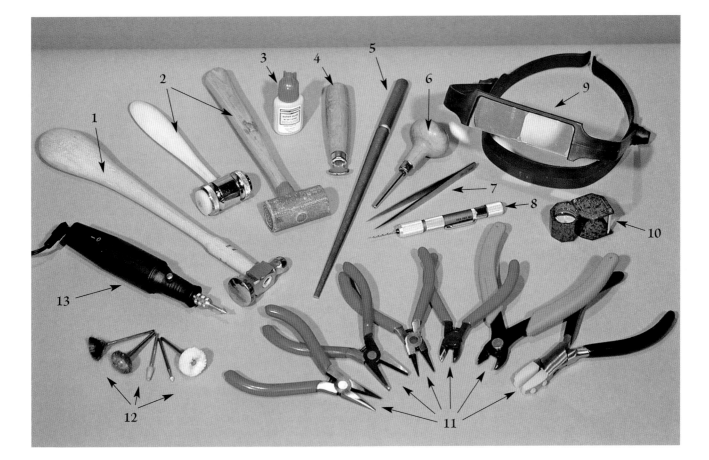

## EMBELLISHMENTS & STONES

1. Fine Silver (.999) Wire - 16, 18, 20 and 28 gauge
2. Lab Grown Gemstones: Corundum and Cubic Zirconia (called CZ's)
3. Findings: Prong-settings for stones
4. Natural Stones
5. Casting Grains: Fine Silver
6. Casting Grains: Brass
7. Casting Grains: Bronze
8. Casting Grains: Gold
9. Necklace chain: available in Fine Silver, Gold, etc.
10. Findings: Silver Pin-backs, Bails, earring loops, etc
11. Beads: available in Fine Silver, Gold, Brass & Bronze
12. Findings: Silver Jump Rings

'Freeform Pendant' silver and 22K gold. The PMC gold element was created and fired first, then lump type silver clay was sculpted around the gold and fired.

*Photo by: Rob Stegman*

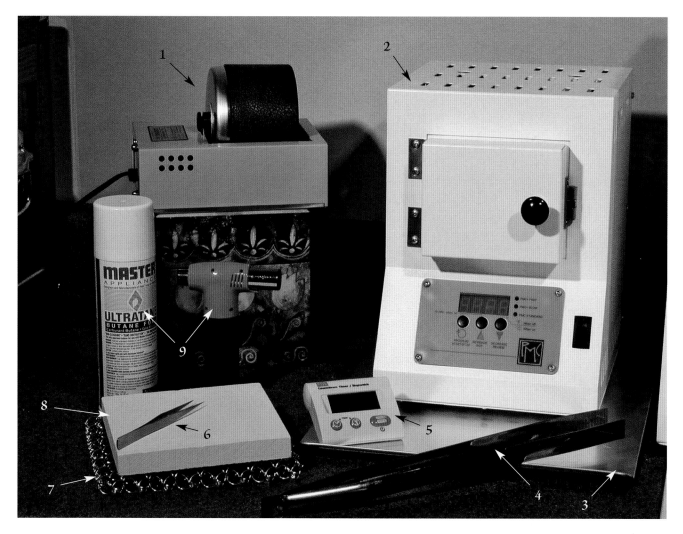

## FIRING & FINISHING EQUIPMENT

1. Rotary Tumble-polisher: with Stainless
   Steel Mixed Shot
2. Small Programmable Kiln: Shown is one of the
   Sierra-PMC kilns that are featured in this book
   but other kilns can also be used successfully
3. Heat-proof Surface, to protect under and in front
   of kiln (insulated cookie sheets work well here)
4. Long Tongs: for removing and placing
   kiln shelves
5. Digital Timer
6. Tweezers: to position items on the kiln shelf
7. Drying Rack: a baker's rack with small
   mesh screen
8. Ceramic Fiber Kiln Shelf
9. Small Butane Torch (right) and Fuel cell (left)

Accessories not shown:
   Ceramic Fiber Blanket
   Pot holders / oven mitts

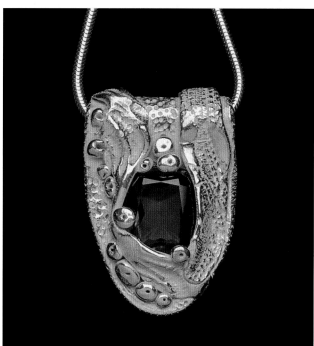

'Sculpted Simplicity' a slab-formed pendant (see project 1, page 21) using a lab grown amethyst. *Photo by: Rob Stegman*

# RING SIZING

We recommend using the PMC+ or PMC3 material for all ring projects. As we mentioned in the 'Types of PMC' material section on page 7 we know these products shrink about 12% from the wet or moldable stage to the finished fired stage. Measuring for a ring using this material must allow for this shrinkage. The least complex way to calculate the effects of this shrinkage is to simply add one (1) size if your making a round band ring, or if your making a larger flat band ring add one and one half (1-1/2) to two (2) sizes. Since the clay shrinks on a percentage basis, the larger the band, the greater the actual shrinkage amount.

We have found this simple method works very well and after finishing a few ring projects you will get very good at estimating the size allowance as compared to the type of ring you're building. If you think you will be making a number of rings all in a specific size you may want to consider purchasing a 'high-fire' ceramic mandrel for one or 2 ring sizes or maybe the entire kit with a full range of sizes (see photo, top right) that is used to both form the ring and hold it during firing. The ceramic mandrel will maintain the diameter of the ring while a special insulation paper (placed on the mandrel prior to forming the ring) allows for the shrinkage and acts as a separator. These mandrels and the special insulation paper are available in kit form from PMC Connection.

Ceramic ring mandrel kit that is used to for both forming a ring and to hold it during firing. The ring cannot shrink during the process because the ceramic mandrel holds the ring's size.

Rings tend to deform slightly during firing. They can easily be reshaped using a steel ring mandrel and a rawhide mallet

# DRYING BOX

You can make a drying box by cutting a hole in one side of a cardboard box sufficient to accept the air discharge vent of a hair dryer. Turn the box onto its side so that the open top now faces forward and the side with the hole is on top.

Place the hair dryer through the top hole. You can improve drying action by placing a small drying rack into the box to hold the PMC pieces slightly above the bottom of the box.

*The Fundamental Clay Shaping Technique, Known as 'Slab-Forming,' Was Used To Create These Extraordinary Slide Pendants With Gemstones.*

# TWO-SIDED TREASURE
## Reversible Textured Pendant

If you look at the back of a piece of fine jewelry you will find that it is as nicely finished as the front of the piece. Many 'Art Jewelers' decorate the back as a reflection of the beauty of the owner. From your first PMC+ piece you can begin to incorporate your designs from front to back. This will give your work a professional quality.

The pendant begins with silver clay rolled into a slab. You then texture the clay and add a stone and other decorations. The size and shape of the pendant as well as the type of texture and decorations can be varied.

## MATERIALS

10-20 grams PMC+ lump clay; PMC+ paste; PMC3 syringe; soda straw; CZ's (Cubic Zirconia) or lab grown gemstones; fine silver or gold casting grains. (Note: PMC3 can be used in place of the PMC+ for this project)

## EQUIPMENT

Programmable kiln, ceramic fiber kiln shelf, 6 playing cards or 2 thickness slats (3/64" / 1.2 mm thick), paintbrush, lace and textured plate, craft knife, tweezers, hair dryer, sandpaper (600 & 1200 grits), stainless steel wire brush, burnishing tool, rotary tumbler with stainless steel mixed shot (optional)

## PROCEDURE

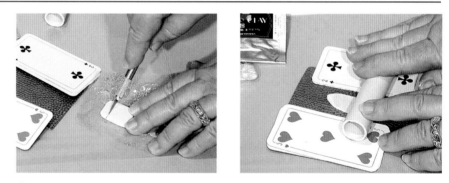

1. Coat your work surface and the textured brass plate lightly with cooking oil (here we are using an organic hand balm salve).

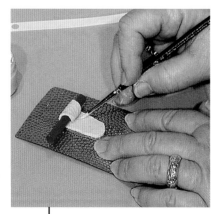

2. Open the lump clay package and cut off a 10-15 gram piece of the clay (about 1/2 to 3/4 of a new package). Be sure to immediately wrap the remaining clay in a small piece of plastic food wrap to keep it from drying out. Lump clay will dry out very quickly if it is not resealed. It can be re-hydrated later with a small amount of water but it is better to get into the habit of keeping any remaining clay wrapped up when not in use.

3. Place two stacks of playing cards (3 cards per stack) on the textured brass plate leaving a 1" (2.5 cm) space between the 2 stacks. Put the small lump of clay in the space left between the cards and place the PVC roller so each end of it is resting on each stack of cards. Now roll the clay flat into the desired shape on the textured plate.

4. The shape of the flattened clay should be roughly 1/2" (1.3 cm) wide by 3" (7.6 cm) long with slightly rounded ends (the exact shape is not critical on this free-form design). Remove the cards and set them aside. Now gently peel the top end of the flattened clay off the textured brass plate and fold it over a soda straw. Open your jar of paste clay and apply a dab of the paste to the joint with a small paintbrush. The paste will act as a bonding agent to secure the seam.

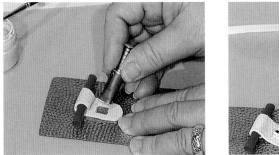 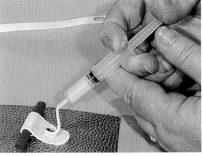 

**5.** We are going to add a gemstone to this pendant but first we want to cut a hole in the area where the stone will be placed. Here we are using a small clay shape cutter that is approximately 1/4" (6 mm) square but you could just as easily use a craft knife to cut this hole. Make the hole slightly smaller and approximately the same shape as the gemstone you have selected. The hole will allow light to pass through the stone, will make the pendant somewhat lighter in weight, and will conserve some of the silver clay material.

Tip: Be sure to recycle the scrap of clay from the cutout hole by adding it back to your remaining lump clay package.

**6.** Gently peel the clay off the metal plate and turn it over to reveal the texture on the front side. Next we'll create the setting for the gemstone. Remove the tip from your syringe clay and extrude a circle bead of clay around the hole high enough to catch the girdle of the stone you have selected (the girdle of the stone is the widest part of the stone). We circled the hole 2 times. Extruding a bead with the syringe will feel a bit awkward the first few times. Try to think of the bead as a piece of wet string and hold the tip 1/2" to 3/4" (1 to 2 cm) away from your work to give the 'string' some freedom to curl and fall into place.

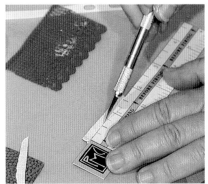

**7.** Don't worry if the extruded bead didn't go exactly where you wanted it (relax, this is your first piece, don't expect perfection). Simply dampen one of your paintbrushes in some water and push the clay 'string' into the shape you desire.

**8.** Pick-up the stone with tweezers, carefully center the stone over the extruded setting you just created and place the stone on the clay. Use the tweezers to gently push down on the stone to both seat it and ensure it is level.

**9.** Now get the playing cards out again and use 2 in each stack to roll the remaining piece of clay flat. Place some lace on the clay and roll gently to put a fancy texture on the surface. Be careful to only press the lace into the surface of clay so it can easily be peeled off.

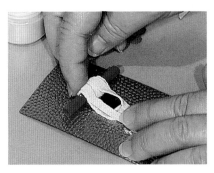

**10.** Cut this textured clay piece into narrow strips each approximately 3/16" (5 mm) wide. We are going to add these strips as decoration to the front side of the pendant. Choose the 2 strips you will use, gather the remaining clay up and seal it away in the plastic wrap and original resealable pouch.

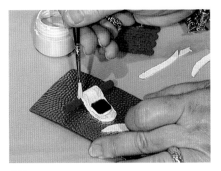 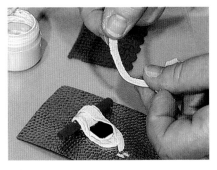 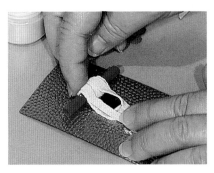

**11.** Once again we are going to apply some paste to act as a bonding agent (glue) to secure the decorative strips to the pendant.

**12.** Place 2 of these strips on the pendant, one on either side of the stone, letting one end drape over the 'soda-straw' and the other end curl toward the bottom center of the pendant.

**13.** Gently press these strips onto the pendant to ensure they are securely attached and have a pleasing artistic appearance.

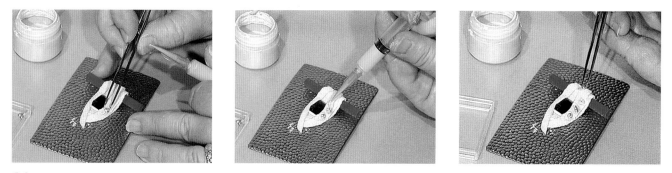

**14.** At this time we are going to affix a few gold casting-grains to give our pendant some color contrast and add interest. Once again we will use the syringe clay to create the settings, but this time we will use the tip attachment with a small hole to run the circle beads of clay. Extrude 2 or 3 small circles of syringe clay (depending on how many grains you want to add). Pick up each casting-grain with the tweezers and press them into the extruded settings.

**15.** The fabrication is complete. Examine your work to make sure the shape is the way you want it and that it has a pleasing artistic appearance. You may want to touch up some rough spots with a dab of the paste clay or add some additional decoration with the syringe clay.

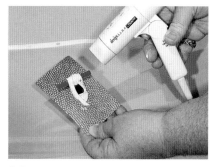

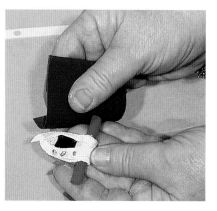

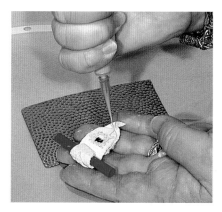

**16.** When you are satisfied with your piece the next important step is to thoroughly dry the pendant with a hair dryer until it is bone-dry. This refers to the condition of the clay after it is completely dried but before it is fired. In this state it is possible to carve the clay using files, cutters and scrapers. It will take some time to completely dry the pendant and you may want to place it in a drying box, electric griddle, or toaster oven (see 'drying box' page 20).

**17.** When the pendant is thoroughly dry it's time to smooth and shape the edges and front side of your piece using a dry sheet of 600-grit sandpaper, then finish sand it with 1200-grit. Depending on the shape and effect you are trying to achieve you could also use jeweler's files, sanding blocks, emery boards or other finishing tools.

**18.** The back of the pendant will have a nice texture that was picked up from the textured brass plate. If your artistic whim tells you to put some additional decoration on either side of the pendant, now is the time to do it. Here I am adding a squiggle of the syringe clay with the fine tip.

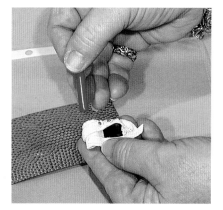

**19.** Be sure to thoroughly dry the pendant again with the hair dryer, (you need to do this only if you've applied some additional decorative touches) and then remove the straw.

**20.** Fire the pendant on a ceramic fiber kiln shelf as directed in addendum 1 page 80.

**21.** Smooth the surface of the fired piece with a stainless steel wire-brush to transform the white surface into a brushed matt finish. Create an artistic contrast with a shiny finish by rubbing the syringe lines with a burnishing tool.

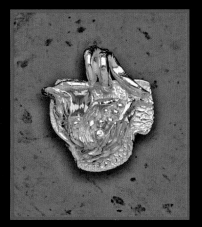

*These Elegant Designs Were Created Using A Basic Clay Shaping Technique Called 'Coil-Forming' The Added Gemstones Elevate Them To The Status Of Fine Jewelry.*

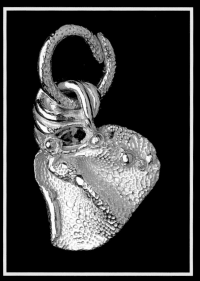

# THE POTTER'S COIL
## Coiled Clay Pendant with Stone Setting

Coil construction is a basic technique from traditional pottery making. We can coil the PMC clay and easily create complex designs, stone settings and bails. The potter's 'coil' will be used in a similar way as the jeweler's 'wire'.

## MATERIALS

20 grams PMC+ clay, PMC+ paste, CZ's (Cubic Zirconia gems), soda straw (Note: PMC3 can be used in place of the PMC+ for this project)

## EQUIPMENT

Programmable kiln, ceramic fiber kiln shelf, paintbrush, hair dryer, sandpaper (600 & 1200 grits), stainless steel wire brush, rotary tumbler with stainless steel mixed shot

## PROCEDURE

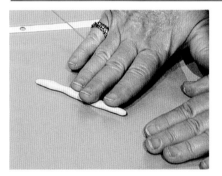

1. Remove the 20 gram lump clay from the package and roll the clay between your palms to create a thick 'coil' (pottery term) roll. Place this thick coil on a smooth plastic or glass surface and continue to work the coil with your fingers keeping it even along the length.

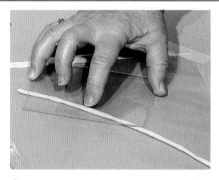

2. It's easier to create an even smooth coil using a flat piece of Plexiglas (or standard glass with the edges ground). Continue to work the coil until it is down to a diameter of about 1/8" to 3/16" (3 to 5 mm).

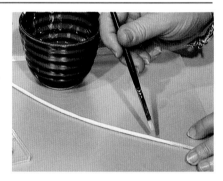

3. Before shaping the coil it is best to brush it with a little water and allow the water to sink into the clay. This will keep the clay pliable and prevent it from cracking.

4. Wrap one end of the coil around the soda straw, looping it two or three times.

5. Place it on a piece of parchment paper (baking/freezer paper) and apply some paste clay with a paintbrush at the coil joints to ensure they will be securely attached after firing.

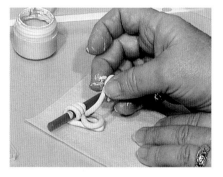

6. Now begin to loop the remaining portion of the coil to fashion an appealing design. Make sure you allow a few spaces in the design for the stones by make small loops slightly smaller than the diameter and about the same height as the stones.

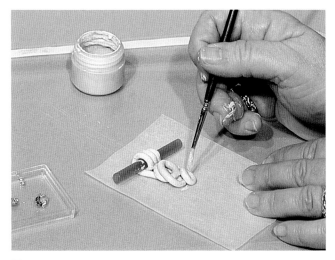

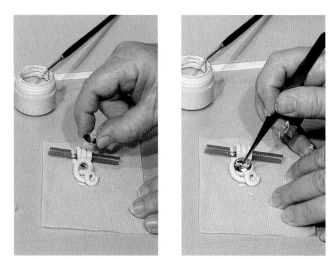

**7.** Use a damp brush to shape the coils and see that the design is well balanced. Use the paste to smooth the surface and make sure the coils are attached to one another. Pay special attention to ensure the coil is firmly attached to the bail loops.

**8.** Set the stones by gently pushing them into the clay so that the clay comes over the girdle of the stone. If the stones are large enough you can place them with you fingers then set them into the clay with tweezers.

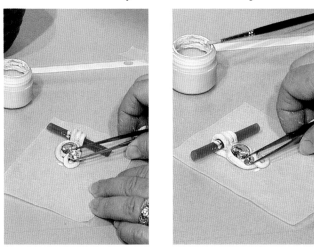

**9.** For smaller stones it will be easier to place them with the tweezers and push them deep into the clay loops until the clay kind of oozes over and around stones girdle.

**10.** Smooth the coils with a damp paintbrush then fill any cracks or undesirable holes with paste.

**11.** Now is the time to add a few gold and/or silver Casting Grains. Make one final inspection of your design. Be sure the stones are completely set into the clay coils and smooth any rough areas with the paste.

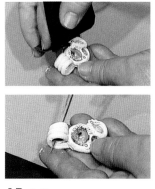

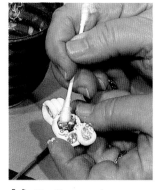

**12.** When you are satisfied with your construction it is time to thoroughly dry it with the hair dryer. Tip: You could place it in a drying box to make this task easier (see page 20 for more details).

**13.** When you are sure your piece has reached the bone-dry state, remove the soda straw and finish all surfaces using files and/or sandpaper (don't forget to smooth the inside of the bail loop with a round file).

**14.** Finally use a damp cotton swab to clean the stones and castings of any clay residue.

**15.** Fire the pendant on the ceramic fiber kiln shelf as directed. See firing chart in addendum 1 on page 80. Finish by smoothing the surface with a stainless steel wire-brush & a burnishing tool to create a contrast.

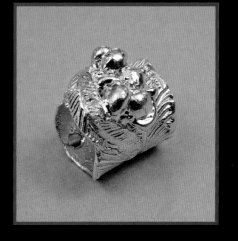

These Cylinder Beads Were Created Simply By Shaping The Silver Clay Around A Burnable Or Removable Core Form, Then Gems And Textures Were Added As A Garnish.

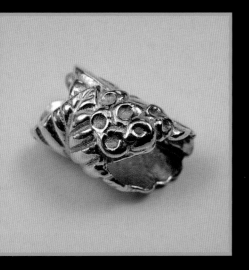

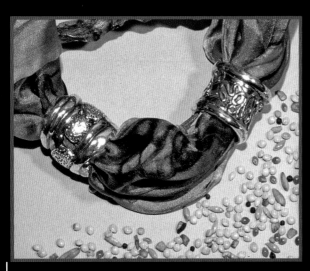

# THE ULTIMATE SCARF BEAD
## Core Formed Cylinder

The cylinder bead is very versatile. It can be formed on a small thin core (e.g. stir straw) and used as a spacer bead or built on a large hollow form core (e.g. cork clay) and used to secure a scarf. Once you have mastered this simple technique you will want to make beads in every size!

Useful core forms are easy to find or make for example: soda straws, bamboo skewers, paper maché, cork clay, wooden dowels, and floral foam to name only a few.

## project 3

## MATERIALS

10-20 grams PMC+ clay (depending on the size of your bead), PMC+ paste, PMC3 syringe, wooden dowel 1/2" (1.3 cm) to 3/4" (2 cm) in diameter, paper, adhesive tape.  (Note: PMC3 can be used in place of the PMC+)

## EQUIPMENT

Programmable kiln, ceramic fiber kiln shelf, 6 playing cards or 2 thickness slats (3/64" / 1.2 mm thick), hair dryer, carving tool, palette knife, clay shape cutters, paintbrush, sandpaper (600 & 1200 grits), stainless steel wire brush, rotary tumbler with stainless steel mixed shot

## PROCEDURE

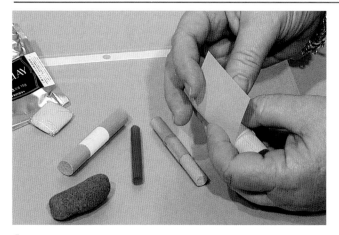

1. Select the bead core you want to use. The photo shows 2 sizes of wooden dowels, a large soda straw and a hand-formed cork clay core. The advantage of using a cork clay core is that you can form it into extraordinary shapes such as an angled or bent bead or one that bumps out in the center. A cork clay core does not have to be removed before firing because cork clay will 'burn out' in the kiln as the silver is firing (see more about cork clay in the Glossary page 10 and in addendum 7 on page 89). If you intend to use a cork clay for your bead you must dry it completely, preferably overnight, before applying the silver clay. For the project we are building here we will use a 3/4" (2 cm) wooden dowel. When using a wood dowel it is necessary to tape a strip of paper around it to allow easy removal of the silver clay bead from the dowel after the piece has dried.

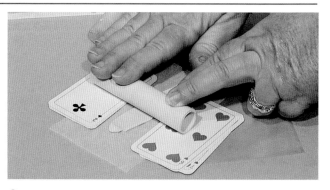

2. Roll the lump clay into a flat sheet using thickness slats (use 2 stacks of 2 or 3 playing cards per stack). The thickness of the clay is based on the size of the tube bead, the larger the bead, the thicker the clay must be.

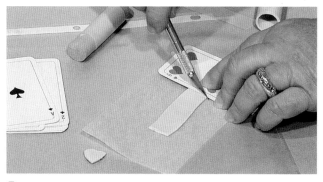

3. Trim the flat clay sheet to the desired width and length.

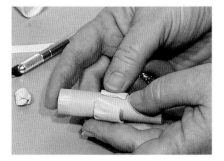

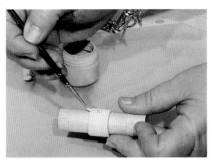

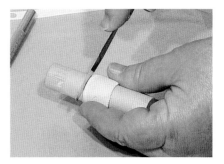

**4.** Wrap the clay strip around the core, trim the ends so they just meet (but don't overlap).

**5.** Then secure the joint with an adequate amount of paste clay.

**6.** Use a flat tool, such as a palette knife, to even the outside edges of the bead.

**7.** Add decorative cutouts or texture to the bead now while the clay is damp. You could use a craft knife for free-form cutouts, or use a one of the clay shape cutters as we are doing here. Note: Clay shape cutters are available in a variety of shapes such as, squares, circles, stars, hearts, etc.

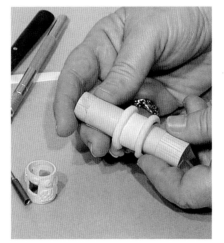

**8.** Once you have the tube bead formed and have added your cutouts or other decorative touches, dry it with a hair dryer. At this point you could call it finished and remove it from the core (note the bead on the left in the photo) or you could continue by adding a coil of clay to both ends to give the bead more structure. To do this roll a long thin coil (see Project 2, steps 1&2) then wrap and attach the coils to the bead ends with clay paste. Finish by drying the coils and the bead. If you wanted to add more decoration to the bead you could add syringe drawings, casting grains or small stones. If you add more decoration be sure to once again thoroughly dry the bead (use the drying box if desired) before removing it.

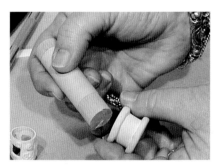

**9.** If you used a dowel as the core remove it now. If you used a 'burnable' core (e.g. cork clay, see page 89) you can leave it in place and it will burn out in the kiln.

## OPTIONS AND OBSERVATIONS:

• Texture the surface with lace, textured plates, rubber stamps, or other texturing tools after you have rolled the sheet in step 2.

• Carve the surface with a craft knife, carving tools or files during step 8.

• Add CZ's with the syringe setting technique. (See page 20 - steps 5 & 6)

• Decorate with syringe work on a solid bead or in cutout areas.

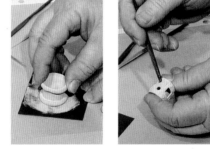

**10.** Put the finishing touches to the bone-dry clay. These photos show smoothing and flattening the bead ends on 600-grit sandpaper and shaping the cutouts with a file.

**11.** Fire the pendant on the ceramic fiber kiln shelf as directed. See firing chart in addendum 1 page 80.

**12.** Smooth the surface of the fired piece with a stainless steel wire-brush to transform the white surface into a brushed matt finish. To create an artistic contrast put a shiny finish on some of the syringe lines by rubbing them robustly with a burnishing tool.

**13.** For a fabulous high gloss polished look, tumble polish your work in a rotary tumbler with a stainless steel shot (see this process on page 86).

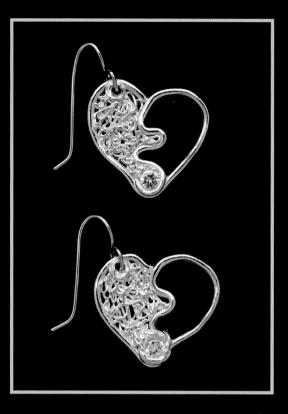

*The Syringe Type Clay Offers The Artist A Unique Ability To Create Intricate Filigree Work That Is As Straightforward As Decorating A Cake.*

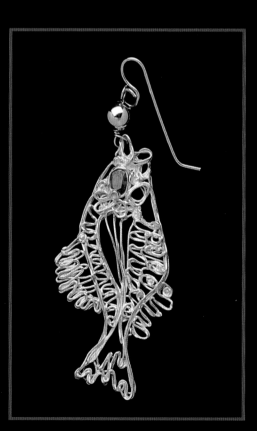

# FILIGREE FISH PENDANT
## 2d Syringe Drawing

Ｉf you like to draw, the syringe is an incredible tool to turn your drawings into pure silver. It will take some practice to learn to control the line of clay as it is squeezed out of the syringe. But the preparation will be worthwhile as you master the art of adding intricate outlines to your work. As you become comfortable with the syringe, you will want to vary the tip size to produce lines of assorted thickness.

## MATERIALS

**PMC+ (or PMC3) paste, PMC3 syringe with tip, drawing paper, cooking parchment or onion-skin paper**

## EQUIPMENT

**Programmable kiln, ceramic fiber kiln shelf, paintbrush, hair dryer, sandpaper (600 & 1200 grits), stainless steel wire brush**

## PROCEDURE

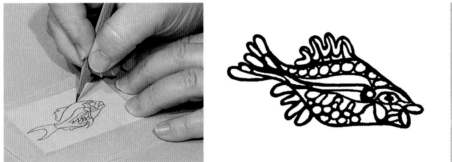

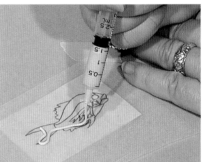

**1.** Begin by creating a line drawing of an object you want to create or select the fish design (above) that we are using as our example for this project. Or you could choose one of the other line drawing designs on page 34. If you're drawing an original design, it is important that all the filigree lines are connected, with no loose ends (loose ends or 'tails' are too fragile, even after firing). Place your design drawing under a sheet of semi-transparent parchment paper, tracing paper, or onion skin paper.

**2.** I always start a syringe drawing by tracing the outline of the design. Use the syringe without the fine tip and begin by extruding about 1/8" (3 mm) then touch the point end of the clay extrusion to the paper to 'lock' this clay string down. Now as you begin to extrude the string slowly lifting the syringe from the paper until you are holding it about 1" (2.5 cm) above the paper.

**Note:** This is a little more difficult than is sounds. It will take some practice to coordinate the speed of lifting the syringe with the speed of the extrusion. If you pull the string off the paper just push it back down with a damp fingertip and continue.

**3.** You will find it easier to control the line if you place your free hand under the syringe hand to act as a support. Apply an even pressure to the syringe to create a continuous line of clay and lay it down as if it were wet string. If you hold the syringe too close to the paper the line will kink and smudge so try to keep the tip away from the work to allow you to move the line with a gentle flowing motion. Remember this first line is only an outline of the fish so don't try to get too fancy with the details just yet. We will come back and add the fins and other details later.

Introduction to Precious Metal Clay

 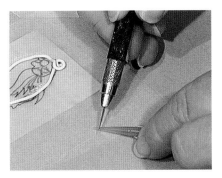 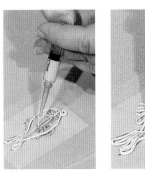

**4.** Continue the extrusion, maintaining one continuous string, until you have arrived back at your starting point. Stop pushing on the syringe plunger and pull the syringe away sharply to break off the string. If the line did not lay down to form the shape exactly as you wanted it (and I would be surprised if it did) you now have an opportunity to move it around. Use a fine point brush damped with a little water to push the clay string into the correct position.

**5.** Next we will go back and add some details. Use a craft knife to trim 1/8" (3 mm) off the small end of the syringe tip to make a tiny 1/16" (1.5 mm) opening (cut only a short piece at first, then check the hole size and cut more if you have to). Screw-mount the tip onto the end of syringe and get ready to use the same extrusion technique as before to create the interior portion of the design.

**6.** This extrusion drawing technique is going to take some practice, so don't get too fussy about your first project. You can push the lines around with the dampened brush and add additional lines as needed later. Use the design drawing more as a guide for your creative inspiration. Remember this is 'hand-made' art with an element of spontaneous creativity.

 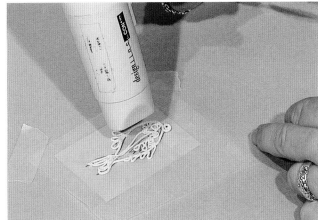

**7.** Dip your brush in water to dampen it and use a little of the paste (or just plain water) to smooth the points, connect the joints and fill in any unwanted cracks or small spaces.

**8.** Dry your extrusion drawing piece with a hair dryer. It will take 5 to 8 minutes to be completely dry and is especially important on this piece due to the thin and delicate lines.

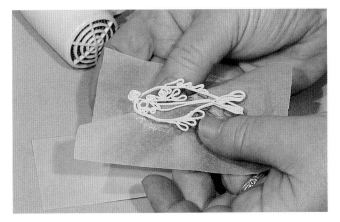 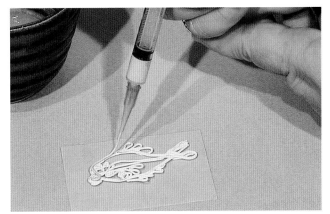

**9.** When you are sure it is completely dry, gently peel the parchment paper off the under side of your piece.

**10.** Now turn the project over and go over the detail lines on the back with another line of syringe clay using the fine tip. This creates a pleasing rounded surface on both sides of the pendant and adds much needed strength. Dry it again.

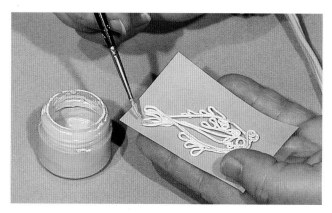

11. Touch the joints with a paste damp paintbrush to secure the ends and to smooth out any rough areas or any small cracks that may have appeared as a result of the handling and drying. You can also fill in small areas with paste if desired.

12. When you are satisfied that your piece is finished, you need to thoroughly dry it with the hair dryer or place it in the drying box if desired. For more information on the drying box see page 20.

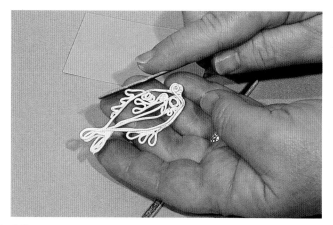

13. Finish by sanding any sharp edges with a fingernail emery board (as shown) or use a sanding block or a small piece of 1200 grit sandpaper.

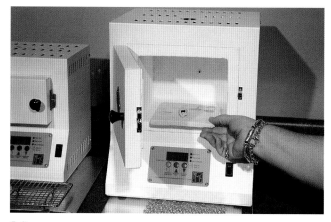

14. Fire the piece on the ceramic fiber kiln shelf as directed.

15. Smooth the surface with a stainless steel wire-brush to transform the white surface into a brushed matt finish then burnish selected areas to create a contrasting glossy finish.

## OPTIONS AND OBSERVATIONS:

I like to think of syringe work in much the same way I think of wirework in traditional jewelry making. The thickness of the clay lines (the wirework) must be proportionate to the size of the pendant. You can vary the thickness of the clay line by having an assortment of syringe tips cut with larger or smaller holes. One note of caution, while you can create a very fine line using the syringe this is going to be a very delicate wire of silver after firing. Be sure to place two or three lines of clay in the areas of greatest stress, or use a thicker line as we did in the outline of our fish pendant.

When the syringe is not in use it is a good idea to keep it nose (tip) down in a container of water to prevent the clay in the tip from drying out. When you are finished using the syringe, remove the tip and put the end cap back on the syringe to keep the clay in the syringe moist and soft. Carefully remove all the clay from the tip and blend it in with the clay in your paste jar. Clean the tip and store it for later use.

*The Variety Of Rubber Stamps Available Today Is Extensive And They Provide A Tremendous Foundation With Imaginative Designs And Textures For You To Use.*

# CALUSA MASK
## Pendant Created with PMC Standard Clay and a Rubber Stamp

The mask design for this project was inspired by the art of the Calusa Indians. This tribe of pre-Columbian natives lived in southwest Florida and their capital city was on an island called Mound Key, very near where I live. I was so impressed with the incredible design work of the Calusa Indians I decided to develop a line of jewelry designs and rubber stamps for our local market.

The mask in this project uses one of my Calusa design rubber stamps, however any rubber stamp design could be used with this technique to decorate a flat silver clay pendant.

This is the only project in this book that uses the PMC Standard clay product. I chose a rather large rubber stamp design to allow for the 30% shrinkage of the PMC Standard and still provide an ample sized pedant for a necklace. Remember when selecting your stamp that the finished piece will be about 70% of the size of the stamp. If you don't want the piece to shrink this much you could use PMC+ lump clay and the shrinkage would only be approximately 12%.

## MATERIALS

**28 grams PMC Standard lump-clay (Note: PMC+ or PMC3 could be used in place of the PMC Std for this project)**

## EQUIPMENT

**Programmable kiln, ceramic-fiber kiln shelf, rubber stamp, cooking oil (or hand balm), 12 playing cards or 4 thickness slats (for total 1/16" / 1.6 mm thick), PVC roller, round coffee stirring straw, hair dryer, sandpaper (600 & 1200 grits), stainless steel wire brush, burnishing tool. Optional: rawhide or plastic mallet, metal 'stake' anvil.**

## PROCEDURE

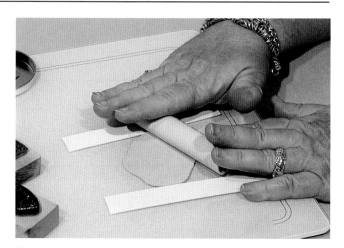

**1.** Coat your work surface and the rubber stamp lightly with cooking oil (or hand balm).

**2.** Open the PMC Standard package and remove the lump-clay. Knead it in your hands for a few seconds to soften it.

**3.** Place two stacks of playing cards, six cards per stack on either side of the clay (we are using matboard slats stacked 2 high for our roller thickness guides) and use your PVC roller to flatten the clay to approximately 1/16" (1.6 mm) thick. Remember this slab is going to shrink by almost 1/3 so it must be thicker than one made from the PMC+ or PMC3 material to allow for the additional shrinkage.

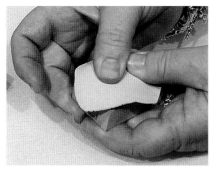

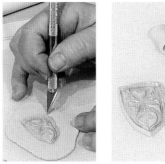
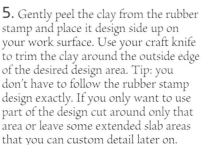

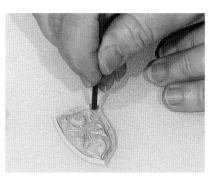

**4.** Pick up the clay slab and place it on the design side of the rubber stamp (you can't see the stamp in my hands because it is underneath the slab of clay). Gently press the clay into the design with your thumbs, applying even pressure over the entire design. This method allows you to see and feel the clay and insure that the design is impressed completely into the clay, but not so far that it weakens the structure.

**5.** Gently peel the clay from the rubber stamp and place it design side up on your work surface. Use your craft knife to trim the clay around the outside edge of the desired design area. Tip: you don't have to follow the rubber stamp design exactly. If you only want to use part of the design cut around only that area or leave some extended slab areas that you can custom detail later on.

**6.** Cut one or two holes at the top of the mask where you will attach the finished pendant to a chain or necklace cord. I like to use a plastic 'stir-stick' straw or similar small tube to push into the clay and open a hole 'cookie-cutter' style. If you want to give your pendant a concave or convex shape simply pick it up and gently shape it with your hands before it is dry. Or you could drape it over an object such as a drinking glass or a rubber ball or into an object such as a plate or saucer. Use you imagination to find something to give it an appealing dimension.

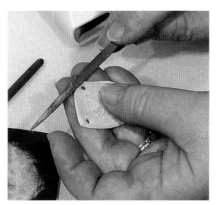

**7.** Thoroughly dry your pendant with the hair dryer (or place it in the drying box if desired). If you used an object to create a shape be sure to leave the pendant on (or in) the object while you are drying it.

**8.** When it is completely dry use files and/or sandpaper to smooth any rough areas and to modify the design as desired.

**9.** Fire the pendant on a ceramic-fiber kiln shelf as directed. See firing chart in addendum 1 on page 80.

**10.** Smooth the surface of the fired piece with a stainless steel wire-brush to transform the white surface into a brushed matt finish. If necessary use a fine jewelers file (as in the photo above) to smooth any rough areas. Then burnish selected areas to create contrasting glossy highlights.

## OPTIONS AND OBSERVATIONS:

Tumble in a rotary tumbler with stainless steel shot if a high polish is desired.

The pendant can be shaped and curved to some extent after it has been fired. Use a rawhide or plastic mallet to shape you pendant over a metal 'stake' type anvil (see addendum 9 page 92).

Apply a patina such as liver of sulfur to create an antique appearance (see addendum 6 - Patina Surface Finishing on page 87).

Use sterling silver jump rings to attach the pendant to a neck chain.

*The Clay-Like Sensitivity Of This Amazing Material Enables The Artist To Easily Transform A Flat Design Into A Three Dimensional Piece Of Jewelry.*

# THE ORCHID
## 3D Stamp Molding Project

This rubber stamp project is similar to the Calusa mask (project 5) in this book but this project is more dimensional and is made by assembling several formed parts. You will learn a technique to capture a design from a flat (2-Dimensional) rubber stamp and create beautiful a 3-Dimensional flower pendant.

The other difference for this project is we will be using the PMC+ material (instead of the PMC Standard). PMC+ is better suited for sculptural forming due to the lower shrinkage factor that holds its shape better during firing requiring only the support of a fiber blanket.

## MATERIALS

**20 grams PMC+ lump clay, 20 grams PMC+ paste clay (Note: PMC3 could also be used for this project)**

## EQUIPMENT

**Programmable kiln, ceramic-fiber kiln shelf, paintbrush, rubber stamp, cooking oil (or hand balm), plastic food wrap, files, clay shaper, hair dryer, sandpaper (600 & 1200 grit), stainless steel wire brush, burnishing tool, rotary tumbler with stainless steel shot**

## PROCEDURE

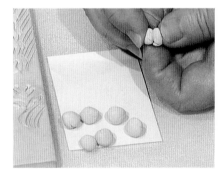

**1.** Select a rubber stamp of an orchid. Use either a commercial stamp or one that you create yourself. It is easy to make stamps from linoleum printing blocks, polymer clay, or even vinyl erasers. I used a rubber printing block and linoleum carving tools to create the orchid stamp for this project. The full-size pattern drawing of my orchid stamp (at right) will allow you to carve your own. These items are available from any art & craft supply stores where you will even find books on stamp making. The stamp will provide surface texture for the flower petals as well as the overall design for your silver pendant.

Prepare the stamp by coating it lightly with cooking oil (or hand balm).

**2.** Count the number of distinct petals in your orchid stamp design. The stamp we're using has six petals. We need to divide the clay into an equal number of small pieces, one for each petal and one for the pendant's bail. Since the bottom petal is much larger than the others, I will allow 2 units for that petal which means I need to divide the clay into eight equal pieces.

**Tip:** roll the clay into a coil about 4" (10 cm) long and cut it into equal 1/2" (1.3 cm) long pieces. As soon as you have made the divisions, roll each one into a ball (between your palms) and quickly wrap them in a small piece of plastic food wrap to prevent them from drying out (notice my little plastic-wrap package in the background of photo 3).

**3.** We will begin our project by forming the bail. Roll one of the clay pieces into coil approximately 1" (2.5 cm) long, (see page 26 step 1 for coil making) and then flatten it slightly with your thumb to make it 1/4" (6 mm) wide. Next loop the coil around a soda straw and join the two ends with a dab of clay paste.

 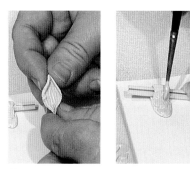 

**4.** Unwrap another piece of clay and roll it slightly between your palms to create a short coil (no more than 1/2" - 1.3 cm), then flatten the coil slightly to create a basic petal shape. Now texturize the clay petal by gently pressing it into the top center petal of the orchid stamp.

**5.** Lift the clay petal out of the stamp and gently shape with your fingers to make it three-dimensional. Join this first petal to the bail using a small amount of clay paste at the joint.

**Tip:** Place a folded piece of paper (or a brush handle) behind this first petal to provide support and maintain the shape of the petal while you're working.

**6.** Repeat steps 4 and 5 for each of the side petals. Remember to apply a small amount of clay paste at the joint for each petal then compress the joint slightly with the end of your brush to ensure the all clay sections are securely affixed.

 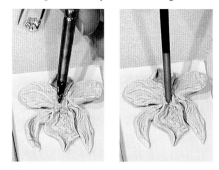 

**7.** Finish the construction using the 2 remaining clay pieces for the larger bottom petal. Apply a little paste, position the final petal then compress the joint slightly with the end of your brush.

**8.** Secure all joints with the clay paste, then use a clay shaper (1st photo above) or the end of a brush (2nd photo) to firmly press the petals into center of the orchid. Also use this tool to refine the shape of the petals and add texture where desired.

**9.** Add a few droplets of syringe clay to the center of the flower to simulate the look of pestles. Or you could add a Cubic Zirconia gemstone to the center (see stone in background) using the syringe extrusion method, as we did in project 2 on page 27.

**10.** Dry your pendant with the hair dryer (or place it in the drying box if desired, see page 20 for details on the drying box set-up).

**11.** When it is completely dry, remove the straw from the bail opening, smooth any rough areas and cleanup or modify the design as desired using files and sandpaper.

**12.** Fire the pendant on the ceramic-fiber kiln shelf cradled and supported in a fibre blanket. Use firing chart temperature and time as directed in addendum 1 on page 80. Polish as desired as explained in previous projects.

## OPTIONS AND OBSERVATIONS:

Can't find a flower stamp and don't feel like carving your own? You can still make this flower by shaping the petals and texturing them with any rubber stamp that has texture lines similar to a flower petal, or use a clayshaper and make your own texture.

Add a professional touch with gold casting grains, or a CZ gemstone (Cubic Zirconia) to the center of your pendant flower. Simply extrude a circle of syringe clay into the center of the flower slightly smaller than the diameter of the stone (or casting grain) you are setting. Then use tweezers to position and gently press the stone into the extruded clay circle until the girdle of the stone is embedded in the clay. For details on this process see page 50, steps 5 & 6.

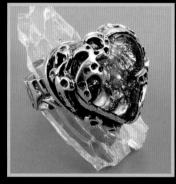

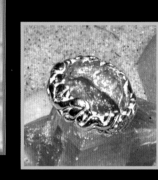

The ability to create a fine silver ring by extrusion is a new phenomenon made possible only with the introduction of this syringe clay material. (Note: Not all rings shown on this page were made entirely from syringe type clay)

# PROMISE RING
## 3d Syringe Ring with 22k Gold Elements

In this project you will learn how to create an extrusion ring and how to incorporate a 22K gold design element plus other decorative touches such as Cubic Zirconia stones, lab grown gemstones, or fine silver components. For this project we will incorporate our own prefered design element made from PMC Gold clay.

The extrusion method is very simple but you must be very careful to dry the ring completely before removing it from the mandrel prior to firing. Alternately you could build the ring on a ceramic ring mandrel and you would not have to remove the ring from the mandrel before firing. (see ring sizing on page 20).

## MATERIALS

PMC3 syringe clay, PMC3 paste clay, PMC Gold clay, and drawing paper.

## EQUIPMENT

Programmable kiln, ceramic fiber kiln shelf, wooden ring mandrel, playing cards (6), texture material, palette knife, hair dryer, paper, sandpaper (600 grit), stainless steel wire brush, burnishing tool, rotary tumbler with stainless steel shot. Optional: Ceramic ring mandrel, special insulation paper

## PROCEDURE

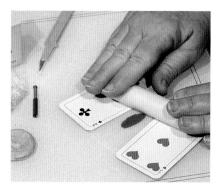

1. The PMC Gold clay component, that we are going to incorporate into this ring design, needs to be created and fired in the kiln by itself prior to placing it into the ring construction. This is because PMC Gold clay requires a higher temperature and longer firing schedule than the silver clay (see firing schedule in addendum 1, page 80). First, plan the design for your gold element for the ring. You could hand-build the shapes with your fingers or roll a small piece of the gold clay into a slab two playing cards thick as I am doing in the photo. Remember to immediately wrap any unused gold clay in plastic wrap and place it in a small zip lock plastic bag.

2. I am going to texture my gold clay slab using a rubber mold I made by pressing an old brass button into a mixture of Room Temperature Vulcanization material (see Mold Making in the Glossary on page 12). You could create your own RTV mold or use a rubber stamp, lace, or any other patterned material. Just as we did with the rubber stamp in project 6, coat it lightly with cooking oil (or hand balm).

3. Press the gold clay slab into the mold with your fingers to give the surface a distinctive texture.

4. Use a clay shape stamp to cut a piece about 1/4" (6.5 mm) square (or round) or use a craft knife to create your element's shape. Cut two additional smaller shapes (about 1/8" - 3 mm) to use as accent pieces.

5. Completely dry the gold clay shapes with the hair dryer (or place it in the drying box if desired).

6. Fire the gold clay shapes at 1830°F / 1000°C for 2 hours (see firing schedule, page 80) and allow them to cool. After the gold shapes are fired and cool enough to handle, you are ready to make the silver portion of the ring.

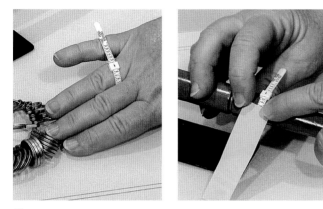

**7.** Determine the ring size you want to make by using a belt type ring sizer (as in the photo) or the traditional ring keys. Now you must add two (2) sizes to the desired ring size. These extra 2 sizes will allow for the clay shrinkage during firing. Use the adjusted ring sizer or the appropriate ring loop to locate the size position on the ring mandrel. Now wrap a small strip of paper around the mandrel, so the center of the paper sits directly on the ring size location, and tape the end of the paper back onto itself. Important note: do not tape the paper to the mandrel or you will not be able to remove the paper (along with the ring) after the clay ring has dried.

**8.** We are going to use all the clay in a new syringe (10 grams) and we are going to use the syringe without the tip. Hold the syringe in your tool hand as shown in the photo and hold the mandrel with your other hand. Slowly extrude the clay from the syringe onto the paper strip. As the clay string flows from the syringe rotate the mandrel while moving the syringe back and forth to create an interesting wavy pattern. It's a bit tricky to extrude the clay, move the syringe and rotate the mandrel all at the same time but it is important to create a continuous band of clay completely around the mandrel (after all that is what a ring is). Continue to extrude the clay, while rotating and moving the mandrel, until the entire syringe is used.

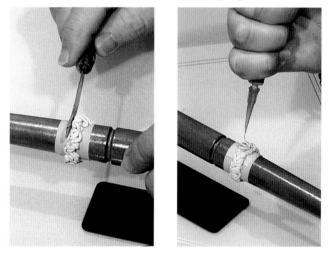

**9.** Dry the ring with the hair dryer until the surface of the clay is no longer sticky (one minute should do it).

**10.** Now we must even out the thickness and edges of the ring. Dampen your fingertip slightly and gently press down on the ring until it is more or less the same thickness around the entire band.

**11.** Use a palette knife (or other flat tool) to gently press in on the sides of the ring until the width is evenly balanced. You may need to press with a damp fingertip and use the knife in combination until you have achieved an attractively composed ring shape.

**12.** The next step is to apply the gold elements. The gold shapes must be seated firmly in the silver clay so that the two metals will fuse during firing. You cannot simply place the gold on top of the silver clay. The best way to do this is to use the small tip on a silver clay syringe and extrude a spiral onto the ring that is about the same size as the gold element.

**13.** Now use tweezers to place the gold element on the extrusion spiral and push firmly to seat the gold element into the still wet silver extrusion.

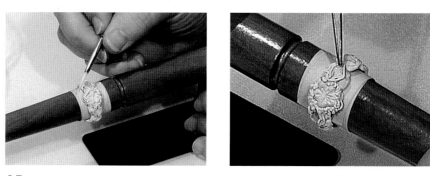

**14.** This photo shows how the ring looks from the side. Notice that the gold element is not sitting on top of the ring but is seated slightly into the extrusion. The ring should be the same thickness all around, push any too-high areas down with a moistened fingertip.

**15.** Set the two smaller accent pieces by either extruding a small dab of syringe clay onto the ring to seat them (as you did with the larger piece) or use some of the paste clay to glue them onto the ring (as I am in the photo).

**16.** Use tweezers to place the accent elements and seat them in the still wet paste clay. Examine your ring and finish the construction by smoothing the surface with a damp fingertip, a damp brush, or perhaps some paste clay to fill in cracks or undesirable spaces. Take the time now to put the finishing touches on your masterpiece.

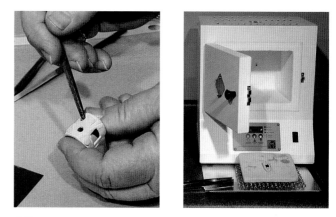

**17.** This time you must place the ring and mandrel into a drying box and let it dry it for at least 1 hour. The ring is very delicate at this stage and will break easily. Do not try to remove it from the mandrel until you are sure it is completely dry. When you confident it is dry, grasp the ring and gently twist the ring along with the paper strip to loosen it from the wooden mandrel. Slide the ring from the mandrel and remove the paper strip from the inside of the ring. Start with the unattached end of the paper inside the coil, which now is exposed, and unpeel it from the dried clay ring.

**18.** Put the finishing touches to the bone-dry clay ring smoothing and shaping it with 600 and 1200 grit sandpaper and/or files as necessary (as we are doing with this bead).

**19.** Fire the ring on the ceramic-fiber kiln shelf at the silver clay temperature and time as directed. See firing chart addendum 1 page 80. Remember the gold has already been fired and will not be affected by the lower temperature of the silver firing.

## OPTIONS AND OBSERVATIONS:

Most items will change shape during firing due to the shrinkage and other factors, however silver is quite soft and can be easily reshaped after firing. If your ring is not perfectly round after firing, simply use a rawhide or plastic mallet and a metal ring mandrel to gently tap the ring back into shape.

You could use gold or fine silver casting grains, Cubic Zirconia, or lab grown stones in place of the PMC gold elements (or in combination).

A set of ceramic ring mandrels is available that can be placed directly into the kiln with you ring construction still on it (see page 20). When using a ceramic mandrel it is not necessary to add 2 sizes to your ring size simply select the mandrel that is the size you need and build your ring. The mandrel must be wrapped with a strip of special high-temp firing paper then the ring is fabricated as described above. Do not remove the ring from the mandrel after it has dried, instead place both the clay ring and the mandrel into the kiln and fire. The fired silver ring will easily slide off the mandrel when it has cooled.

**20.** After firing, smooth the surface with a stainless steel brush to create a matt finish. Use a burnishing tool to produce a high shine surface (as I am doing in this photo) or for an all over high gloss polished look, tumble polish your work in a rotary tumbler with a stainless steel shot (see details of this process on page 86).

*A Burnable Core Form - Including Natural Leaves - Enables Jewelry Artists To Make A Wide Range Of Hollow-Form Shapes From Tiny Tea Pots To Miniature Bird Houses*

# THE ANCIENT VESSEL
## Hollow-Form Shape Technique

project 8

This project will teach you how to make large, lightweight hollow-forms using a burnable core and the paste type clay. The traditional jeweler's technique of hammering, forming and soldering the precious metal components to produce the desired shapes is no longer necessary. Use this technique to create almost any shape of hollow form.

This project is called an 'Ancient' vessel because we are going to use 'liver of sulfur' (sulfurated potash) antiquing solution to prematurely age the silver surface and create a patina.

## MATERIALS

7-10 grams PMC+ lump clay, 10-20 grams PMC+ paste clay, PMC3 syringe clay, cork clay (for hollow form), CZ's (Cubic Zirconia) or lab-grown stones.

## EQUIPMENT

Programmable kiln, ceramic-fiber kiln shelf, paintbrushes, hair dryer, stainless steel wire brush, burnishing tool, liver of sulfur (sulfurated potash).

## PROCEDURE

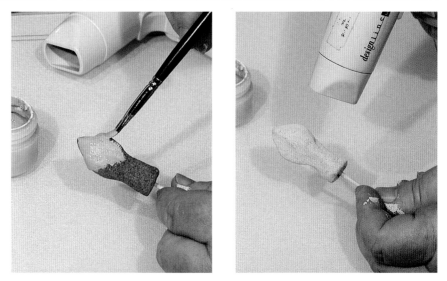

1. Use a piece of cork clay to create the core form in the desired vessel shape with your fingers. For this project I want a rather odd shaped jug form. Stick a toothpick in the end that will be the vessel opening to help you hold onto it during fabrication. For more on cork clay turn to page 89.

2. The cork clay must be thoroughly dry before proceeding onto the next step; this will take at least 12 hours of air-dry time. If the inside of the cork clay is still moist when coated with the paste clay, moisture will be trapped inside. During kiln firing the expansion of the water vapor will crack the silver layer.

3. Paint the surface of your cork clay shape with one thin coat of the paste type clay using a small brush. Dry this first coat with the hairdryer. Apply a second thin coat of paste clay to your project and dry it. Continue to build up the thickness using this process until you have applied 7 or 8 coats of paste (final coating thickness should be a minimum of 1/32" / 1mm ). You should increase the number of coats for a larger vessel.

Note: Turn to addendum 7 on page 89 for more information on core forming materials that are organic and safe to burn.

 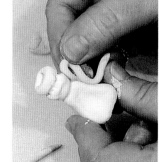  

**4.** Make two short coils using the lump clay to form the handles for our vessel. Apply some paste to the coils in the areas where they will contact the vessels.

**5.** Join the coils to the dry vessel by pressing with your fingers and adding more paste where needed.

**6.** A clay shaper is used to texture the handles and ensure they are pressed firmly to the vessel.

**7.** Finish the handles with some paste to smooth the surface and fill in any cracks or spaces between the handles and the vessel.

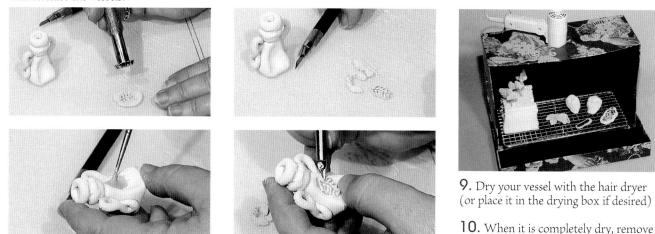

**9.** Dry your vessel with the hair dryer (or place it in the drying box if desired)

**10.** When it is completely dry, remove the toothpick from opening, smooth any rough areas and cleanup or modify the design as desired using files and sandpaper.

**11.** Fire the piece on the ceramic-fiber kiln shelf as directed. See firing chart addendum 1 page 80.

**8.** Next we will decorate the surface with added clay shapes. Here I am using a leaf patterned, leather stamping tool. I used a small piece of lump clay that I flattened slightly with my thumb and pressed it into the clay (remember to coat the stamper with oil). I then cut the leaf shape with a craft knife, put some paste clay on the vessel to act as my glue, and finally pressed the leaf into the paste with a clay shaper to make sure it was firmly attached. Note: I could have used decorative syringe work, added some CZ's or many other variations to put a decorative finish on this vessel.

## OPTIONS AND OBSERVATIONS:

The cork clay will create smoke as it 'burns out' during the firing process. Place the kiln in a well-ventilated area. Do not panic and open the kiln door when smoke appears. This action provides oxygen and could result in a sudden flash of flame from the kiln chamber.

Be careful to coat the shape evenly with the paste clay. Any thin areas may crack during firing. If this happens simply fill the crack with more paste clay and re-fire to close the crack.

This burnout core technique can be used to make many different hollow form shapes. In addition to the ancient vessels, another favorite of mine is miniature 'Old Birdhouses'.

**12.** Brush part or the entire piece with a stainless steel wire brush. Burnish part or all of the brushed areas. If you leave some of the white surface and then antique it with liver of sulfur, the white areas will take on an 'ancient clay' look. Careful contrasting colors in the oxidation process can make this project look like a real archeological find! Turn to addendum 6 on page 87 for step-by-step instructions on using liver of sulfur to add an antique patina.

Hand-Made Papers, Natural Fabrics Or Other 'Burnable' Items Such As Leaves, Seeds or Flowers Can Be Coated With The Paste Type Clay To Create Unique Designs.

# PAPER ALCHEMY PENDANT
## A Free Form Paper Brooch

Making hand made paper is a passion of mine. Now you can capture the wonderful natural contours of the paper in pure silver. (Note: handmade papers can be purchased in art & craft stores). You can create free form designs using textured paper or use origami paper folded to create a one of a kind silver sculpture. The range of possibilities is almost unlimited. You can use most organic materials such as plant seeds, tree leaves, flower buds etc. or natural fiber fabrics such as cotton or linen.

## MATERIALS

PMC+ paste, PMC3 syringe, handmade paper, 3" to 4" (7.5 to 10 cm) long piece of 18 gauge silver wire (.999), CZ's (Cubic Zirconia) or lab grown stones

## EQUIPMENT

Programmable kiln, ceramic-fiber kiln shelf, paintbrush, stainless steel wire brush, burnisher, tweezers, liver of sulfur

## PROCEDURE

1. Tear a piece of handmade paper into an interesting shape then crumple or form the paper into the shape you desire. Dip the paper in a bowl of water to moisten it.

2. Make a loop on one end of the silver wire to be used as the bail. Thread the wire through your paper leaving the loop end exposed just enough to get a neck chain or cord through it.

Note: If you intend to use this piece as a brooch you do not need to add this bail wire. The brooch pin should be added later using the soldering technique described in addendum 4 on page 85.

3. Use a small paintbrush and a liberal amount of the paste clay to carefully coat the front surface of the paper project. Make sure to get the clay paste completely into all of the crevices and folds.

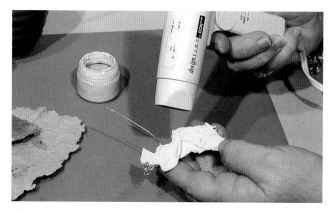

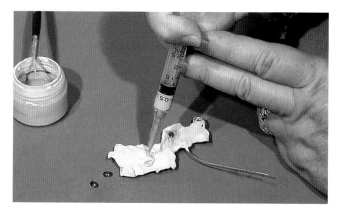

**4.** Dry the front side of the piece with the hair dryer, then coat the backside with paste clay. You should have 3 to 4 coats of paste on each side. Be sure to dry the piece well between coats. The paste should be 1/64" (.5 mm) thick on each side, for a minimum total of 1/32" (1 mm) plus the paper thickness.

**5.** Next we will strategically place some stones in and around the folds. I am using small lab grown, smooth oval stones for my project, but you could use CZ's in any shape you would like. Use the tip on the syringe and extrude a circle of clay sufficient to capture and hold the girdle of the stones.

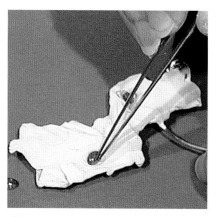

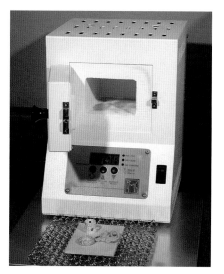

**6.** Use tweezers to carefully place the stones in the extruded clay circle and gently push them down to ensure they are fully seated. Feel free to add as many stones, CZ's or syringe decoration, as you desire.

**7.** Dry your pendant with the hair dryer (or place it in the drying box if desired, see page 20 for more details).

**8.** When it is completely dry smooth any rough areas and cleanup or modify the design as desired using files and sandpaper.

**9.** Fire the pendant on the ceramic-fiber kiln shelf as directed. See firing chart in addendum 1 on page 80.

**10.** Smooth the white surface residue with a stainless steel wire-brush that will give your piece a brushed matt finish. To create an artistic contrast try putting a shiny finish on some selected areas by rubbing them with your burnishing tool. Or apply an antique patina using liver of sulfur (see page 87).

## OPTIONS AND OBSERVATIONS:

This paste clay coating technique works fantastically well on leaves, pine tree cones, maple tree 'keys' or any other natural plant fiber (you could even coat dead insects, like a large beetle). Most importantly, the core that you are coating must be safely 'burnable' so it will turn to ash during the firing and leave only the fine silver shell that mirrors the shape and texture of the original item.

If you are coating a tree leaf it is only necessary to coat one side and I recommend that you coat the underside. Most leaves have a much more pronounced and interesting texture pattern on the underside and that textured side will become the top-side of your jewelry piece.

Sterling silver findings (.925 silver) need to be soldered on after you have fired the silver clay piece (see addendum 4 on page 85 for soldering techniques). During kiln firing, Sterling silver will develop a fire scale that darkens the metal surface. This will happen even at 1110°F / 600°C, the lowest temperature used to fire the silver clay. This discoloration is difficult to remove and may weaken the structure of your piece.

Add Precious Metal Silve
Clay Ornamentation An
Syringe Lace Decoratio
To Pre-Fired Ceramic an
Porcelain Components T
Open A Whole New Worl
Of Possibilities.

Pottery Vase (at right) & Covered Box (upper left), were created by: Vera Lightstone

Porcelain Doll created by: Helen Tickal

All PMC silver embellishments were created by: Mary Ann Devos

# PORCELAIN DOLL ARM BRACELET
## Syringe Extrusion Lace Decoration

If you or someone you know has a passion for making or collecting fine porcelain dolls this technique is a natural match. Add beautiful fine silver jewelry to enhance these dolls with tiny bracelets, necklaces and finger rings all designed and fired directly on the doll's delicate arms, fingers or neck. The jewelry can be made in any style from Victorian to Modern. Sculpted pieces and ornate syringe lines can be further enhanced with CZ's (Cubic Zirconia) or lab grown corundum stones.

## MATERIALS

Bisque fired doll necks, arms or legs (colored, fired and ready to be mounted on the doll), PMC3 syringe clay, PMC+ lump clay, PMC+ paste clay, Cubic Zirconia or lab grown stones.

## EQUIPMENT

Programmable kiln, kiln shelf, texture material, fiber blanket (to support the ceramic during firing), fiberglass brush, burnishing tool, hair dryer.

## PROCEDURE

**1.** First we will create several tiny textured ornament components to add to the jewelry. Roll a thin slab from lump clay using only two playing cards on each side of the clay to maintain an even thickness. Texture or mold the clay using lace, rubber stamps or any other texturing device and cut several small element shapes.

**2.** For this doll bracelet I am going to use some lace to texture the surface. Then I will cut four small petals shapes that I will use to form a flower. Apply a tiny amount of paste to the back of one of the petals and place it on the dolls wrist. Do the same for the remaining 3 flower petals.

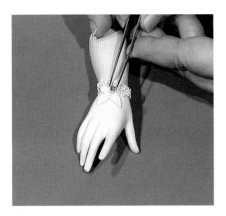

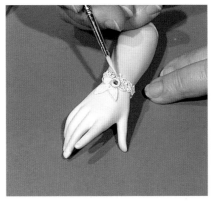

**3.** Put the small tip on the syringe and begin to extrude a line of clay, creating small 'lace-like' loops that run completely around the arm of the doll. This will look like a silver band or chain. If you wish you could modify the diameter of the line by cutting the end of the syringe tip with a craft knife. Make sure the syringe lines are connected all the way around the doll's wrist. As the clay shrinks during the firing it will 'shrink-lock' the silver to the porcelain.

**4.** Use the side of a damp brush to push the extrusion flat onto the porcelain surface and to ensure the extrusion are attached to one another.

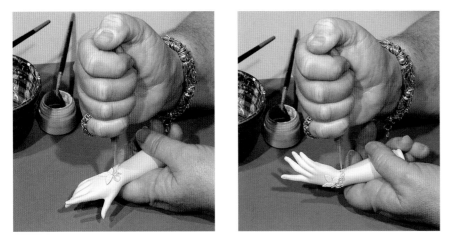

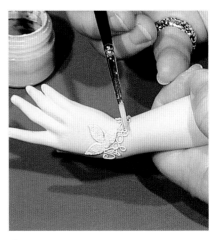

**5.** Next add a stone to the flower center. Extrude a circle of syringe clay slightly smaller than the stone and use tweezers to place the stone in this circle. Press the stone into the clay until the clay is above the girdle (widest portion) of the stone. As the clay shrinks it will hold the stone firmly in the clay.

**6.** Finish the piece with a little paste to smooth the stone setting, the flower petals and the lace bracelet. When you have completed the bracelet, dry with a hair dryer and check to ensure all of the elements are secure. Important tip: Be sure to use a cotton tipped swab to clean off any residue clay particles or smudges. If these are left on they may be impossible to remove after firing.

**7.** Fire the doll parts on the ceramic fiber kiln shelf, using fiber blanket for support. Since you are firing porcelain along with the silver clay this time, you should ramp up the kiln at 1000° F / 535° C per hour, fire it for 30 minutes at 1470° F / 800° C and cool very slowly (do not vent the kiln).

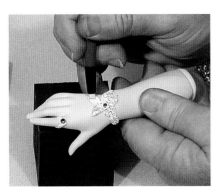

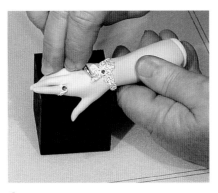

**8.** Smooth the white surface on the silver using only a fiberglass brush Do not use a stainless steel brush, as it will leave marks on the porcelain.

**9.** Use the burnishing tool to bring some selected areas to a high polish.

## OPTIONS AND OBSERVATIONS:

The same technique can be used to add silver details to doll necks, fingers, or other areas.

Use your imagination to visualize many other ceramic or high fire pottery items that would be enhanced with the addition of silver decorative details.

Turn to project 13 on page 60 of this book for another idea to decorate a glazed porcelain photo frame and an elegant cake server.

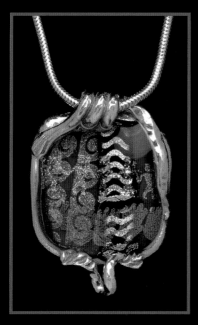

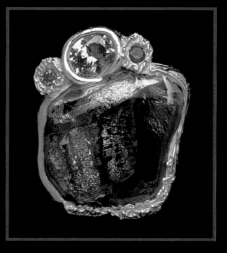

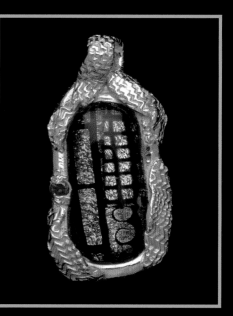

*Fused Glass Goes Together Perfectly With The Silver Clay Material. A Style Of Art Glass Called 'Dichroic' Has A Gemstone-Like Quality That Is Nothing Short Of Stunning When Merged With Fine Silver.*

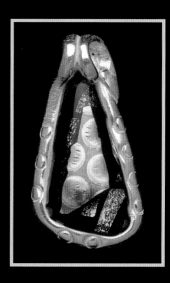

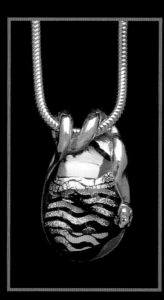

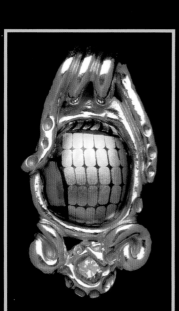

# DICHROIC GLASS PENDANT
## Fused Glass And Silver Clay In Combination
### project 11

One of the most exciting things to do with this silver clay material is to combine it with fused dichroic glass cabochons. The beauty of the glass and the fine silver settings make exquisite one-of-a-kind pieces. You can use any type of fusible glass to combine with PMC.

## MATERIALS

10-20 grams of PMC+, PMC+ paste, PMC3 syringe, dichroic glass cabochon (make them yourself or purchase them from art glass stores or jewelry suppliers), PMC Connection glass firing paper (or similar product)

## EQUIPMENT

Programmable kiln, ceramic-fiber kiln shelf, shelf release 'glass firing' paper, paintbrush, stainless steel wire brush, and burnishing tool

## PROCEDURE

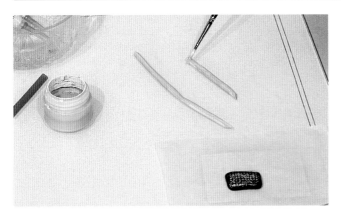

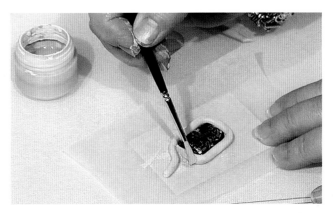

1. Dichroic cabochons combine beautifully with fine silver to make magnificent pendants. Select a glass cabochon that is a suitable size and shape for the pendant you want to make. I like to carefully and thoroughly clean the glass cabochon now and try to keep handling to a minimum as I work. Silver clay dust plus the oils from your hands will fire into the glass and leave a permanent blemish. It's important to keep the glass pristine! Roll the lump clay between your palms to create a thick coil. Then use a flat piece of Plexiglas (or standard glass with the edges ground) to work the coil until it is down to a diameter of 2/3 the height of the cabochon (about 3/16" - 4.8 mm). Use a damp brush to moisten the clay coil and allow a few seconds for the moisture to sink into the clay.

2. Place the cabochon on a piece of parchment paper and wrap the coil around the cabochon to encircle it. The ends of the coil should meet at the top of the pendant. Overlap them slightly and join them using a dab of paste.

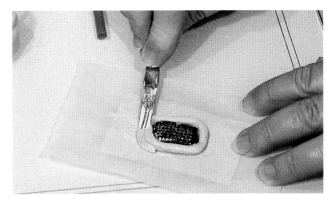

3. Press down with a pallet knife to ensure this seam is secure. This clay ring is called the 'safety circle' and will prevent the glass and silver from cracking during firing.

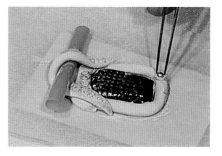

**4.** Use the remaining coil for the bail loop. Apply paste to secure one end of the coil to a top corner of the pendant. Place a soda straw across the top and bring the other end of the clay coil over the straw and attach it to the opposite top corner with a dab of paste clay.

**5.** You could put some decorative marks on this bail coil using a potter's tool or any sharp stick but do not put any decorative marks on the safety coil around the glass. Marks in the safety coil create weak points that could break during firing.

**6.** Alternatively you could add some gold or silver casting grains (as I am doing), or decorate the piece with more coil loops or ornamental syringe work.

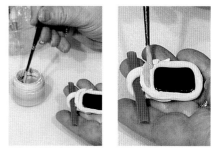

**7.** Clean the glass with a cotton-tipped swab dipped in denatured alcohol to remove fingerprints or other grime that could fuse into the glass during firing.

**8.** Dry your pendant with the hair dryer (or place it in the drying box if desired)

**9.** When it is completely dry, remove it from the paper, turn it over and fill the coil joins with some of the paste. Dry it again and finish the construction by smoothing any rough areas using 1200 grit sandpaper.

**Note:** Do not cross over the glass with the silver clay, paste or syringe work. Putting the clay on the glass may cause it to crack during firing and will stain the glass with a hazy 'burnt' pattern.

## OPTIONS AND OBSERVATIONS:

**10.** Firing a piece that incorporates a glass cabochon requires a slightly different procedure. First you must place a sheet of shelf release paper on the ceramic-fiber kiln shelf and place your pendant on this paper to preserve a smooth finish on the back surface of the glass. Place the shelf with your pendant in the kiln. Increase the temperature at a moderate rate, about 1500°F/ 816°C per hour. Fire the piece to 1110°F / 600°C and hold that temperature for 45 minutes.

**11.** Since we fired the PMC to only 1110o F / 600o C, it is possible simply to allow the pieces to cool, with the kiln door closed, to room temperature. Glass is most sensitive below 1000° F/ 535° C, so it important to allow a slow cooling below this temperature level. Do not open the kiln during this cooling. If firing to a higher temperature, it may be advisable to "crash cool" the glass to 1000 o F/ 535 o C by opening the kiln door. (See addendum 1 – page 81 for more information on firing glass items.)

**12.** When the glass is cool, the silver can be polished using the stainless steel wire brush and burnisher. These brushes will not damage the surface of the glass.

Clear glass may acquire a faint yellow halo as it reacts with the fine silver during the firing process. This stain will only appear at the areas where the clear glass and silver meet. This 'silver staining' is a normal reaction. If you use a cabochon with dichroic colors or one with a solid color glass at the perimeter edge (where the silver touches the glass) you can avoid this halo effect.

Do not attempt to use the PMC standard clay with glass. Standard clay shrinks 30% during firing and this shrinkage will stress the glass and will likely cause it to crack.

Photo by: Speedy Peacock

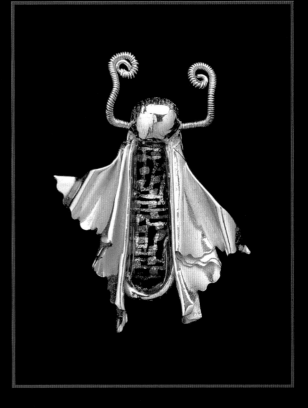

*Sheet-Type Clay Combines Splendidly With Fused Glass, Ceramics or even Wood To Create Unique Designs.*

# KAMAMA BUTTERFLY PIN

## Sheet Type Clay with a Dichroic Glass Cabochon

KaMaMa is Native American Cherokee language for butterfly. The butterfly is the universal symbol for rebirth and transformation into splendor and Precious Metal Clay truly is the rebirth of silver. This project was created for a series of classes presented in Japan in April 2001 and is dedicated to the Japanese artists who shared this experience with us. You can use this technique as a starting point to make any winged creature, bug, bird or bat.

## MATERIALS

10 grams PMC+ lump clay, PMC+ paste clay, PMC+ sheet clay, a dichroic glass cabochon, 5"(12.5 cm) length of 18 gauge fine silver (0.999) wire, 72" (1.75 m) length of 28 gauge fine silver (0.999) wire, shelf release 'glass firing' paper, white glue, Sterling silver or stainless steel pin back finding, epoxy glue (Note: PMC3 can be used in place of the PMC+ for this project)

## EQUIPMENT

Programmable kiln, ceramic fiber kiln shelf, paintbrush, stainless steel wire brush, burnisher, rotary tumbler, round nose pliers, decorative craft scissors and paper punches

## PROCEDURE

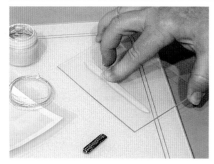
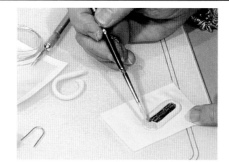
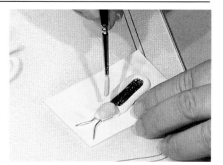

1. Select a glass cabochon that is the size and shape to use as the butterfly's body (about 1" x 1/2" - 2.5 x 1.3 cm). Roll the 10 grams of lump clay between your palms to create a thick coil then use a flat piece of Plexiglas (or standard glass with the edges ground) to work the coil until it is down to a diameter of 2/3 the height of the cabochon (about 3/16" - 4.8 mm). Use a damp brush to moisten the clay coil and allow a few seconds for the moisture to sink into the clay.

2. Place the cabochon on a piece of parchment paper and wrap the coil around the cabochon to encircle it. The ends of the coil should meet at the top of the pendant. Overlap them slightly and join them using a dab of paste. You've just created a safety circle (see project 11, step 3).

3. Shape the antennae by bending the 1 mm / 18 gauge wire into a 'U' shape. If you intend to hang the finished piece as pendant, form a second loop on the inside of the 'U' (see sketch below left) by wrapping the wire around a small paintbrush handle. Place the wire on the clay circle at the top of the cabochon and paint a small amount of paste over the wire where it touches the clay.

4. Now place a small ball of clay over the paste and wire to form the butterfly's head. The ball of clay will hold the wire in place and the paste will help the two clay bodies adhere.

5. The rest of the piece will be completed in the bone-dry clay state. Dry your butterfly head and body with the hair dryer (or place it in the drying box if desired).

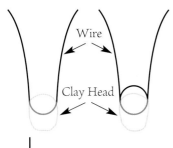

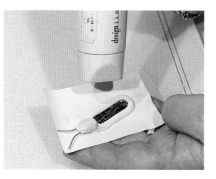

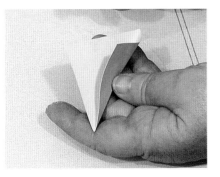  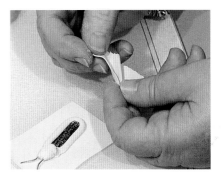

**6.** Fold the 2-1/4" (5.7 cm) square sheet in half to make a triangle. Cut the sheet diagonally along the crease to make 2 triangles. Separate these triangles and fold them in half again to make 2 smaller triangles.

**Note:** See project 18 on page 78 for more techniques on using the sheet type clay.

**7.** Use the serrated craft scissors to trim the long side of the triangle adding a decorative edge. Repeat this procedure for the other triangle. Since the sheet type clay is so thin you must keep the triangle shapes together to make the wings double thick.

**Tip:** Recycle the sheet type scraps and cutoffs. Even though the sheet type clay feels different, it is compatible with the PMC+ paste and will re-hydrate nicely.

**8.** Now put some decorative folds the triangle shapes to give them a wing-like appearance. You will find it very helpful to place a tiny amount of white glue at the top of the folded seams to hold them in place after you have folded them.

**9.** Add some paste to the side of the safety circle and some along the lower wing edge and attach this wing the body section.

**10.** Repeat this same procedure for the other wing.

**11.** Dry your KaMaMa thoroughly with the hair dryer (or place it in the drying box if desired, see page 20). Sheet type clay contains no water and will not become hard as it dries.

 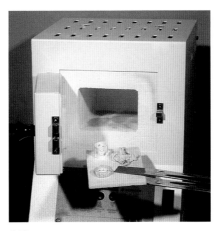

**12.** Clean the surface of the glass with a cotton-tipped swab dipped in denatured alcohol to remove all fingerprints or other grime that could fuse into the glass during firing.

**13.** Fire this piece following the same procedure we used for project 11 steps 10, 11 & 12 on page 56. Also refer to the firing chart and additional kiln information in addendum 1 on page 80.

## OPTIONS AND OBSERVATIONS:

I like to finish my butterfly's antennae by wrapping or winding the 18 gauge wire with a very fine 28 gauge silver wire (I used this 'wire winding' technique extensively for the mask shown in the photograph on page 8). I think it gives the antennae a very authentic look.

Curl the ends of the antennae into a natural butterfly shape using round-nose pliers.

Finish the brooch by attaching a pin-back to the back of the glass body using 2 part epoxy.

Add Distinctive
*O r n a m e n t a l*
*Elements To Fine*
*Porcelain Such As*
*Serving Utensils,*
*Picture Frames, Tea*
*Cups or Any Other*
*Porcelain Item That*
*You May Choose To*
*Brighten Up.*

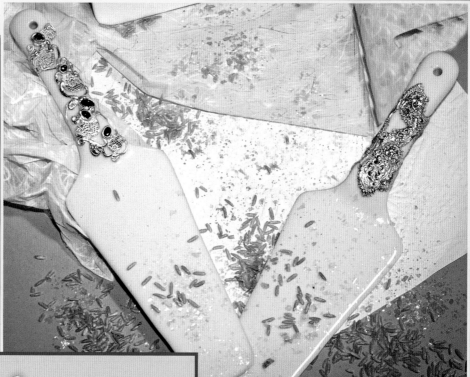

# COMMEMORATIVE SERVER
## Decorated And Bejeweled Fine Porcelain

Use this silver clay material to add distinctive ornamental elements to fine porcelain. Create a beautiful gift for special occasions such as weddings, anniversaries, retirement, etc. For this project we will use the 12% shrinkage of the PMC+ material to our advantage and use it to 'shrink-lock' the silver decoration to the porcelain during the firing process.

## MATERIALS

6 grams PMC+ lump clay, PMC3 syringe clay, glazed porcelain spoon or cake server, 2 or 3 Cubic Zirconia stones

## EQUIPMENT

Programmable kiln, kiln shelf, playing cards (4), texture material, fiberglass brush, burnishing tool, tweezers, hair dryer

## PROCEDURE

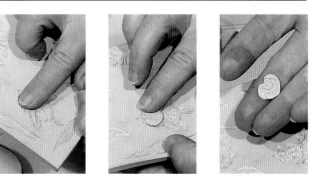

1. First we need to design several small textured ornaments for our decoration. Roll a thin slab from lump clay using only two playing cards on each side of the clay to maintain an even thickness. Cut several small element shapes using 2 or 3 different sizes and shaped stamp cutters or simply freeform cut with your craft knife.

2. Add texture to these element pieces using a texture mold (as I am doing here) or use some lace, assorted rubber stamps, or any other texturing device.

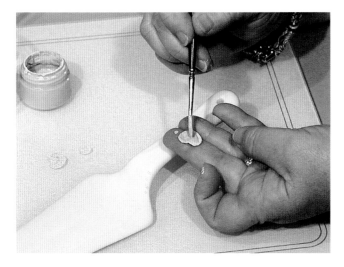

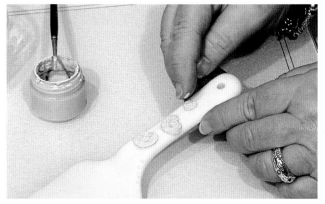

3. Apply a tiny amount of paste to the back of one of the textured ornaments and place it on the handle of the spoon or server. Do the same for any remaining ornament pieces.

**4.** Hold the porcelain utensil and use the syringe clay to carefully draw an extrusion design all the way around the handle. Be sure to incorporate the already applied textured ornament pieces in this design (they will not stick to the porcelain on their own). For this project I find it is best to use the syringe without the tip because lines that are too thin could break or come loose if the server was ever actually used. Be sure all syringe lines are connected and there are no loose ends. The clay will shrink about 12% in the firing and that is just enough to hold the decorative tracery firmly to the porcelain.

**5.** When you have your syringe design complete (don't forget you can move and shape it a little bit using a damp brush), dry the clay on the serving utensil with a hair drier only until it is no longer sticky. Plan where the stones will be set. You could use one of the loops of syringe work already in place, provided it is deep enough to hold the girdle of the stone. Or you could add some syringe circles to make the connection between the stones and the rest of the design especially strong. The area where a stone is set is a stress point within the overall design, so make sure there is enough syringe tracery to hold the stone and keep the design together.

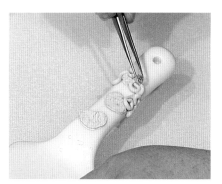

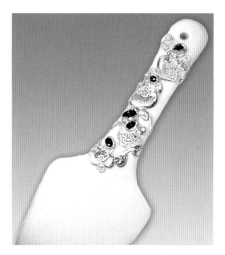

**6.** Dry your porcelain item thoroughly with the hair dryer (or place it in the drying box if desired, see page 20). When it has dried, clean any excess silver (smudges of paste, etc.) from porcelain surface without the use of moisture. The powdered residue will simply brush off using a cotton-tipped swab.

**7.** Fire the piece on a ceramic fiber shelf using a fiber blanket to support porcelain items in the kiln. Ramp the kiln up at 1000°F / 535°C per hour and hold at 1470°F / 800°C for 30 minutes. Cool slowly.

**8.** Smooth the white surface of the silver with a fiberglass brush for a matt finish (we're using the fiberglass brush on a porcelain doll arm in photo above right). Accent the design with areas of high shine silver using the burnishing tool.

**Tip:** After firing, if you find a syringe line or two that are not fully attached do not despair. Simply extrude a little more syringe clay to cover the gap, dry (with hair dryer), clean (as before) and fire the item again.

## OPTIONS AND OBSERVATIONS:

For wedding parties: a set of porcelain serving utensils can be made using Cubic Zirconia stones that are the color of the bridesmaids' dresses (if that is possible to find). The style of the work can reflect the theme of the wedding. This makes a wonderful keepsake that is one of a kind and very personal.

For anniversary gifts: Make a porcelain photo frame using Cubic Zirconia birthstones for the celebrants.

New Baby Keepsake: A porcelain photo frame using the Cubic Zirconia birthstone of the new baby.

Birthdays, graduation, retirement, the gift ideas are unlimited.

*Natural Gemstones Are Mounted In These Pieces Using Conventional Bezel Mounting Techniques.*

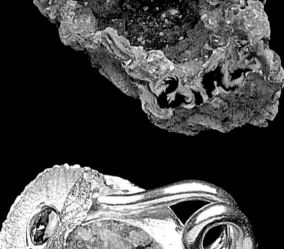

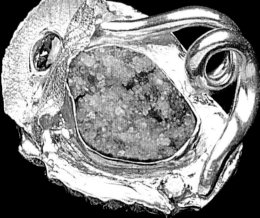

# NATURAL STONE SLAB RING
## With Fine Silver Bezel Setting

Fine silver bezel wire can be used to set natural stones which would be damaged during the firing process. Use this technique to make findings for all of your natural stones in pendants, pins or earrings.

## MATERIALS

20 grams PMC+ lump type clay, PMC+ paste type clay, PMC3 syringe type clay, fine silver (0.999) bezel wire, natural stone cabochon

## EQUIPMENT

Programmable kiln, ceramic fiber kiln shelf, ring sizer, ring mandrel, playing cards (18), hair dryer, flat jeweler's file, sandpaper (600 – 1200 grit), files, craft knife, self-adhesive note sheet, wire brush, burnishing tool, rotary tumbler with stainless steel shot

## PROCEDURE

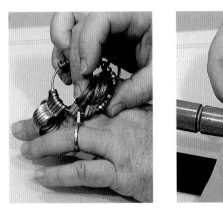
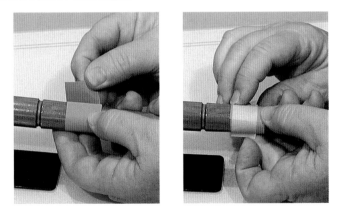

1. Measure for the correct ring size, then add 2 sizes for a flat band ring to allow for the 12% shrinkage when the PMC+ material has been fired (see Project 7 page 43 - steps 7 & 8 for more details on ring sizing allowance).

2. Place a small strip of paper on the ring mandrel at the appropriate size.

3. I like to use the 'removable self-adhesive' note paper for this, however you must be sure to start wrapping the note strip from the non-adhesive end, then the finishing end will have the tacky strip to secure the paper back onto itself.

4. I also like to secure the paper further using a small piece of adhesive tape, just to be sure it stays put. However it is important that the paper is not taped to the mandrel.

5. Use 20 grams of lump type clay to create a slab that is 3/64" (1mm) to 5/64" (2 mm) thick (use 3 to 6 playing cards for thickness spacers) A ring band needs to be a minimum of 3/64" (1mm) thick for a delicate design look but could be up to 5/64" (2 mm) if you're making a more substantial design (don't forget this clay will shrink by 12% when finished). Cut a strip as wide as desired for a flat band ring. I'm going to use 3 playing cards to make mine 3/64" (1mm) thick and trim it to 5/16" (8 mm) wide. Remember to gather up the left over pieces, roll them into a ball and seal them back in the plastic bag ASAP.

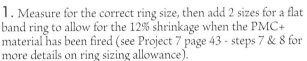

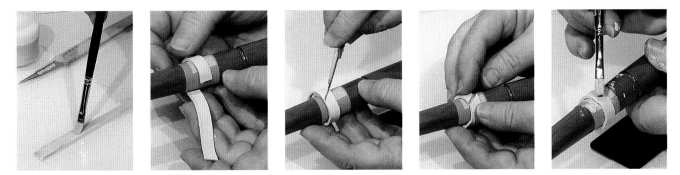

**6.** Moisten the clay strip with some water on a brush before wrapping it around the paper strip on the mandrel. Overlap the ends of the clay band and cut through both layers (at a diagonal) with the craft knife. Remove both cut off ends and secure the resulting 'butt-end' joint with a little paste clay. The strength of the joint will be improved by adding a bit more paste clay to the joint area.

**7.** I like to brush a little paste clay on the surface around the entire ring circumference. This adds a bit more silver material for strength and augments the 'hand-made' look.

**8.** Dry the ring on the mandrel to the bone-dry clay state. Do not remove the ring band yet. Simply smooth the outside surface with fine sandpaper (not too much sanding) and set it aside for now.

**9.** The next step is to create a fine silver bezel to fit precisely around the cabochon. Bezel wire is available in many sizes and styles. Typical sizes are 26, 28, & 30 gauge by 3/32" (2.4 mm), 1/8" (3.2 mm), or 3/16"(4.8 mm). In addition it can have a plain top edge, or the edge could be serrated, scalloped or other pattern (see examples of these in the photo above). Whichever you choose the bezel height must be high enough to capture the stone, plus you must allow some additional height for the portion that will be embedded into the silver clay base. A good rule of thumb is to choose a bezel wire that is 1/32" to 3/64" (0.8 to 1.2 mm) higher than necessary to capture the stone.

**10.** Wrap the fine silver bezel wire around the cabochon (position the joint on a long side of an oval stone) and mark the place where it joins up. Remove the cabochon and cut the wire using flush cutting pliers with the flat face toward the piece being cut. File the ends until you have a snug fit with an even joint.

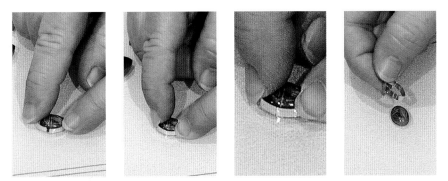

**11.** Now test the bezel size by placing it on a flat surface then drop the stone into the bezel. Make sure that the ends come together around the stone with no gaps between the stone and the bezel. Pick up the bezel to verify that the stone releases easily with no binding.

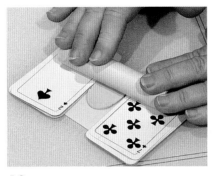

**12.** Roll out another piece of lump clay and make this one 1/8" (3 mm) thick, (spacers would be 9 cards high). This will become the base on which the stone will rest.

**13.** Place the bezel on this new base and gently press it about 1/3 of the way into the 1/8" (3 mm) thick slab. Do not push the wire too far into the clay slab. Pushing the wire too far into the clay will thin the clay under the wire, possibly causing the clay to split during firing. Also, since the wire does not shrink with the clay during firing, there could be some distortion of the clay slab around the wire. Use your craft knife to cut around the bezel. Do not cut it flush with the bezel but leave a little clay all around. You could add a fancy cut pattern to the edge of base if you would like. Use your artistic whim and have a little fun.

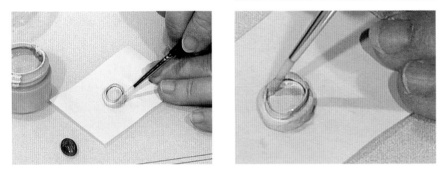

**14.** Now paint several coats of paste around the base of the embedded wire on the outside of the bezel, filling in the space left next to the wire when it was pushed into the clay slab. Also apply some paste at the joint in the bezel, both inside and out. Dry thoroughly between each coat of paste.

**15.** Dry the bezel and base assembly until it has reached the bone dry stage. Finish it with sandpaper and/or files as needed.

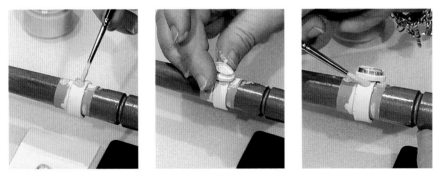

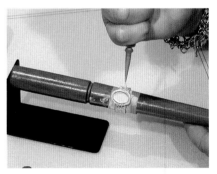

**16.** We're ready to fasten our base and bezel to the ring band. Apply a liberal amount of paste clay to the band directly over the joint area. Put a little paste on the underside of the bezel base and place it on the band. Take some care to ensure the bezel is level, square and positioned exactly the way you want it. When you're satisfied add some paste to fill in the spaces between the band and the bezel to ensure it will be solidly attached.

**17.** Add some syringe decoration to the band (if desired) or embellish the setting with small CZ (Cubic Zirconia) stones or castings grains (review this procedure in project 1 on page 24 steps 14 & 15). Be careful that you do not place any silver elements too close to the bezel. You will need to be able to bend and shape the bezel after firing to set the stone into the bezel.

**18.** Thoroughly dry the ring on the mandrel, then gently remove it and finish it inside and out with fine sandpaper and/or files as necessary.

**19.** Fire the ring on the ceramic-fiber kiln shelf, supported on a ceramic fiber blanket, at the silver clay temperature and time as directed. See firing chart in addendum 1 on page 80.

**Note:** Do not fire the ring with the natural stone set in the bezel. Most natural stones cannot withstand the high temperature of the firing.

**20.** After firing smooth the white surface with a stainless steel brush to create a matt finish. Use a burnishing tool to produce a high shine surface. For an all over high gloss polished look, tumble polish your ring in a rotary tumbler (see photo above) with a stainless steel shot (details of this process on page 86). You may choose to put a patina on the ring then remove the patina on some areas to add an interesting feature.

**21.** The final step is to set the stone. Place it into the bezel so that it lies flat on the base (as you had it when you created the bezel). Be sure that the stone does not rock within the bezel. If it does, the base is not flat. You must flatten the base inside the bezel or you will risk cracking the stone. Apply a small amount of epoxy or other strong adhesive inside the bezel prior to inserting the stone.

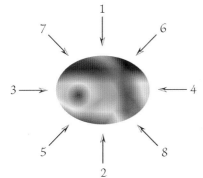

**22.** Use a bezel pusher to smoothly bend and flatten the bezel around the cabochon to conform to the cabochon's curving surface. Begin on one side of the stone and push in on the bezel then move to a point directly opposite and repeat the process. Turn the ring 90 degrees (midway between the first two points) and repeat the process then move to a point directly opposite the third point and repeat. Continue this process moving back and forth (as shown on the diagram above) until the bezel is tight to the stone.

**23.** Finally smooth the bezel surface against the stone and remove any irregularities using a burnishing tool.

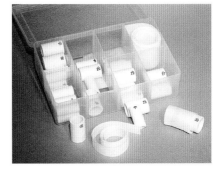

**Tip:** Use a ceramic ring mandrel to prohibit the shrinkage during firing. These mandrels can be placed directly into the kiln with the fabricated ring mounted on it. This set of mandrels is marked with metric ring sizes.

## OPTIONS AND OBSERVATIONS:

If the ring (band)is not perfectly round after firing, simply use a rawhide or plastic mallet and a metal ring mandrel to gently shape the ring. Note: Be sure to do this prior to setting the stone in the bezel but you must be careful that you do not bend the bezel while hammering.

A set of ceramic ring mandrels is available (see photo at left) that can be placed directly into the kiln with your ring construction still on it. When using a ceramic mandrel it is not necessary to add 2 sizes to your ring size. Simply select the mandrel that is the size you need and build your ring. It is necessary to wrap the mandrel with a strip of special firing paper then fabricate your ring as described above. Do not remove the ring from the mandrel after it has dried but place both the clay and the mandrel into the kiln and fire. The fired silver ring will easily slide off the mandrel when it has cooled.

*To Create Your Own Clasp Findings*
*...ther  Decorative  Components  To*
*...e Your Jewelry Creations With Style.*

# ORNAMENTAL NECKLACE CLASP
## Slab Formed Components Made
## With Fine Silver Wire

Pᴍᴄ+ and PMC3 silver clay combines perfectly with fine silver wire. Clasp designs can be simply a functional component of your work or you can create elaborate sculptural clasps that are a work of art in their own right. Make ornamental clasps for beadwork necklaces, bracelets or other jewelry creations.

## MATERIALS

Lump type clay, Paste type clay, 16 gauge fine silver wire (.999). Optional: CZ's (Cubic Zirconia) and syringe clay

## EQUIPMENT

Programmable kiln, ceramic fiber kiln shelf, slats, craft knife, brass plates, pattern cutters, rubber stamps, hair dryer, burnisher, wire brush, tumbler with stainless steel shot

## PROCEDURE

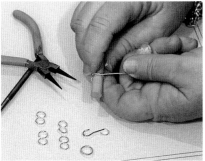

**1.** Use a 5/16" (8 mm) diameter dowel to shape a 'hook-with-eye' from fine silver wire (see full-size diagram above). Give the hook a finished look by using a small torch (refer to addendum 4 - torch soldering on page 85) to melt the end of the wire to create a small sphere. Or simply file the end of the wire to remove the bur and fold over the last 1/16" (1.6 mm) of the wire (see diagram). This will double the wire at the end and form a smooth, rounded tip. Make a figure '8' (double-loop) for the catch end of the clasp, leaving the open part at one of the ends. The diagram above provides full-size patterns for these 2 wire components (including the alternate tip).

**2.** Coat a textured brass plate with hand balm (or cooking oil).

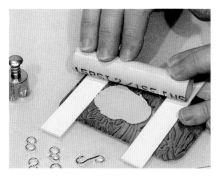

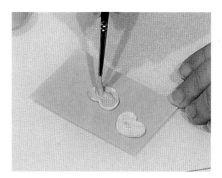

**3.** Place the clay on top of the brass plate and use thickness slats to roll a slab 3/64" (1 mm) thick.

**4.** Cut the slab into a shape with a pattern cutter, (I'm using a heart cutter). Make four identical shapes; we need 2 pieces for the hook side of the clasp and 2 for the eye side.

**5.** Turn one of the slab shapes pattern side down and coat this 'inside' top surface with a little paste clay.

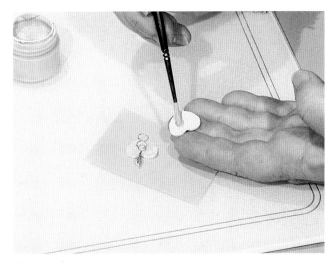

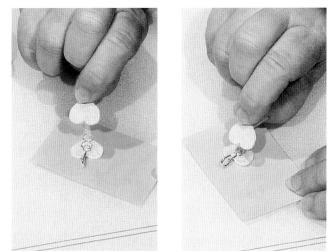

**6.** Now place the wire components on the clay slab in the desired position. The hook (with eye) component will form the clasp and figure '8' will be the catch that will to hold strand of beads together. Use pliers to put a 1/4 turn on the hook. Then place the hook so that the portion that extends beyond the clay is perpendicular (90°) to the base.

**7.** Coat another clay slab with paste clay and sandwich the wire parts between the patterned cut pieces. Gently press the sandwiched assembly together then use some paste clay to fill the edge gap and make it smooth. Repeat this process for the 'eye' end of the clasp. Be sure to place the 'open end' of the figure 8 piece inside the clay sandwich.

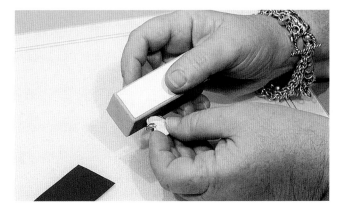

**8.** Dry the pieces completely to a bone dry state using a hair dryer or the drying box as we have done before. Another idea that works very well with flat pieces like these clasps is to use an electric griddle or frying pan. Be very careful to set the temperature on low to gently heat the pieces (after all you don't want to 'fry' them).

**9.** When the pieces have reached the bone-dry clay state, use fine sandpaper or a sandpaper buffer block (as shown) to smooth and finish the edges and surface.

## OPTIONS AND OBSERVATIONS:

Adding CZ's (Cubic Zirconia) or casting grains using the syringe clay setting technique could further enhance these clasps.

Sterling silver wire can be used in place of the fine silver wire. If you use sterling silver in your PMC3 projects it should be fired at 1110o F / 600o C for 45 minutes. In addition you will need to use at least 16 gauge sterling wire as thinner wire has a tendency to weaken and break after firing. There usually will be some fire scale on the sterling as the copper component in the alloy burns on the surface. This can be sanded off and polished in the tumbler or the piece could be antiqued with liver of sulfur. For details on this antiquing process see addendum 6 on page 87.

**10.** Fire the clasps on the ceramic fiber kiln shelf as directed. See firing chart in addendum 1 on page 80.

**11.** Polish with a wire brush or place in a stainless steel shot tumbler. The tumbler will 'work-harden' the fine silver wire, making it a little stiffer (see addendum 5 - page 86).

Introduction to Precious Metal Clay

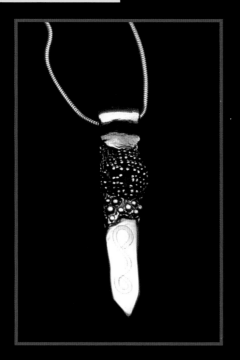

*Brass Screen And Wire Combines With This Silver Clay Material To Easily Create Exciting Mixed Metal Sculptures.*

# SCREEN IMAGERY PENDANT
## Brass Screens Add Depth and Interest

### project 16

Stainless steel or solid brass screen can be fired with PMC+ to give your work a contrast in color and pressing the clay through the screen will produce a magnificent texture. This project is really creative and lots of fun to do.

## MATERIALS

20 grams PMC+ lump clay, 20 grams PMC+ paste, 10 grams PMC3 syringe, solid brass screen, brass tubing 1/8" to 3/16" (3.2 mm to 4.8 mm) diameter, solid brass fish charms or other brass component design of your choice. Note: Be sure to use solid brass screen and components only as brass plated objects will not survive the firing process

## EQUIPMENT

Programmable kiln, ceramic-fiber kiln shelf, paintbrush, stainless steel wire brush, burnisher, rotary tumbler, round nose pliers, decorative craft scissors and paper punches

## PROCEDURE

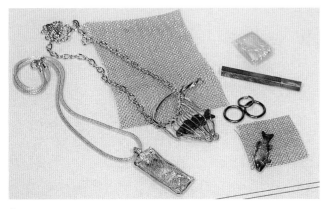

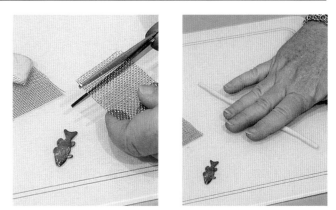

1. The first step is to plan your design. The photo shows a couple of necklace pendants I made using brass components, plus a selection of components that I could use for this new design. I need to make a pendant that I can use to decorate the cover of a hand-made photo album. I have decided to attach a 2" (5 cm) length of 1/4" (6.5 mm) square brass tubing to the hanging bale, simply as a design element.

2. Cut the solid brass screen into a square that is approximately 1-1/2" (3.8 cm).

3. Roll the lump clay into a coil that is approximately 3/16" (4.8 mm) thick.

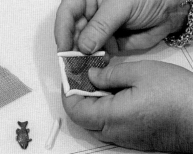

4. Cut four pieces from the coil to match the sides of the screen. Press each coil piece onto the side edges of the screen. Make sure the raw screen edge is covered. Use a bit of paste clay at the corners to secure the corner joints between the coil pieces.

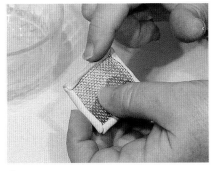

**5.** Use a wet finger to smooth the coil frame edges and secure corners. Dry the frame pieces (with the hair dryer) so they will stay put as you continue to work on the design.

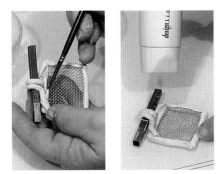

**6.** Use another length of coil to attach the screen frame to the brass tubing. Brush some water onto the coil and wrap it around the tube then use paste clay to attach the coil to the screen frame. Dry the piece again.

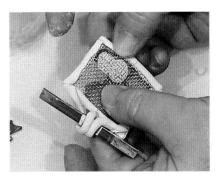

**7.** Make 2 or 3 small balls from lump clay 1/4" (6.5 mm) diameter and push them through the screen from the back. It's important to leave enough clay on the backside to secure the clay. The front side will have 3D design effect.

**8.** Shape 2 or 3 pieces of lump clay into the seaweed elements and texture them using a piece of lace (or other textured surface).

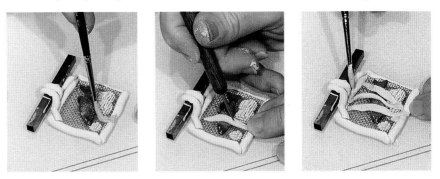

**9.** Use paste clay to attach a small lump of clay to the backside of the fish. Place the brass fish component on the screen and push the attached clay into the screen to secure. Now overlay the seaweed elements attaching them to the screen frame with paste clay and gently push the top sections into the screen to secure (use a clay shaper as shown). Finish by applying some paste clay to any weaker areas or to fill in gaps.

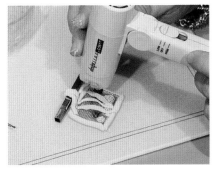

**10.** Dry the piece with a hair dryer until it can be safely handled. Turn the piece over and add some paste clay or small pieces of lump clay to ensure all the elements will fuse to the screen during firing. Now finish drying the piece completely to the bone-dry state. You can use the hair dryer, the drying box or the electric griddle.

**11.** Once the piece is completely dry you should finish the surface and touchup any rough areas.

**12.** Fire the brooch on the fiber kiln shelf as directed. Refer to firing schedule in addendum 1 on page 80.

**13.** After firing clean the pendant with a wire brush. If you have difficulty removing the fire scale from the brass components, you could try soaking the piece in jeweler's pickle solution (see page 12). If desired, you can polish in a rotary tumbler with stainless steel shot.

## OPTIONS AND OBSERVATIONS:

You could use stainless steel screen or design components instead of the solid brass or mix them in the same piece to add contrast and interest.

This project design can be further enhanced with antique patina, using liver of sulfur or similar agent.

*PMC3 Silver Clay, With Its Lower Firing Temperature, Presents A Bouquet Of Possibilities For The Jewelry Designer To Incorporate Even More Fused Glass*

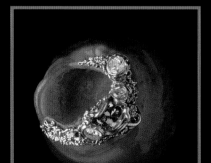

# MILLEFIORI PENDANT

## PMC3 with Millefiori (A Thousand Flowers) Cabochon

PMC3 type clay fires to pure silver at a lower firing temperature than any of the other clay types. The lower firing temperature of 1290°F/ 700°C (for 10 minutes) or 1110°F/ 600°C (for 45 minutes) is below the full-fuse melting point of glass. This provides a welcome opportunity for us to use tack-fused glass in our work while maintaining the 3-dimensional look and feel. In addition we can use the lower firing colored glasses, patterned decal transfers, iridized glass and cabochons made from patterned rod and Millefiori slices. Most of these accessories are damaged or distorted at the higher temperature required when firing standard or PMC+ type clay.

## MATERIALS

**10-20 grams of PMC3, dichroic or millefiori cabochon (make them yourself or purchase them from art glass stores or jewelry suppliers)**

## EQUIPMENT

**Programmable kiln, ceramic-fiber kiln shelf, shelf release 'glass firing' paper, paintbrush, stainless steel wire brush, and burnishing tool**

## PROCEDURE

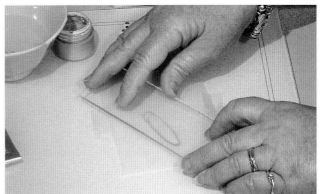

**1.** Fused glass cabochons combine faultlessly with the PMC 3 material due to the low kiln firing temperature required. Select a glass cabochon that is a suitable size and shape for the pendant you want to make. Remember to carefully and thoroughly clean the glass cabochon now and try to keep the handling of the glass to a minimum. Remove the PMC3 from the package and roll the lump clay between your palms to create a thick coil.

**2.** Use a flat piece of Plexiglas (or standard glass with the edges ground) to work the coil until it is down to a diameter of 2/3 the height of the cabochon (about 3/16" - 4.8 mm) then moisten the clay coil with a little water.

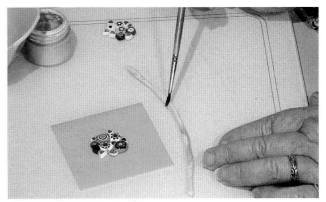

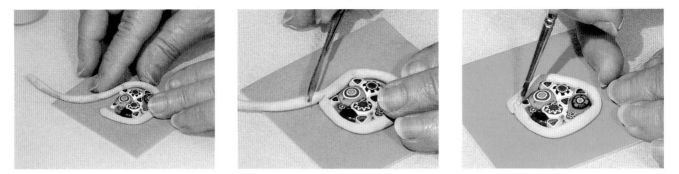

**3.** Place the cabochon on a piece of parchment paper and wrap the coil around the cabochon to encircle it. The ends of the coil should meet at the top of the pendant, cut the coil, overlap the ends slightly and join them using a dab of paste.

**4.** Cut three pieces from the remaining coil and roll each one into a ball. Apply some paste and arrange them at the top corner of the pendant.

**5.** I'm going to add a CZ by placing it on the center ball and then embedding it into the clay with my tweezers until it has gone past the girdle of the stone. Alternatively you could add gold or silver casting grains.

**6.** Add a final decorative touch using a leather-craft texturing tool to enhance the clay-coil border. Be sure to texture the surface only. Do not press too deep or scribe any lines into the coil as this may weaken the safety circle and cause it to break during firing.

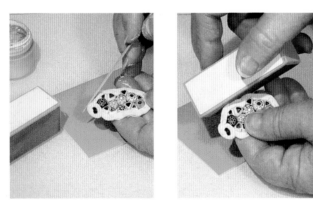

**7.** Clean the surface of the glass with a cotton-tipped swab dipped in denatured alcohol to remove all fingerprints or other grime that could fuse into the glass during firing. Then dry the pendant with the hair dryer (or place it in the drying box if desired).

**8.** When it is completely dry shape the design with a jeweler's file and smooth the sharp edges with 1200 grit sandpaper or an emery block as I am doing here.

**9.** After the pendent is fired and cooled it can be polished using the stainless steel wire brush and burnisher. Or for a high polish look, place it in a rotary tumbler. The steel shot will not damage the surface of the glass.

## OPTIONS AND OBSERVATIONS:

Remember that any jewelry piece incorporating a glass cabochon requires a slightly different firing procedure. Please review the firing process for project 11 steps 10, 11 & 12 on page 56 and the firing schedule information in addendum 1 on page 80

The firing temperature of PMC3 is lower than the melting point of glass and that unleashes a number of new possibilities for creative designing. One of the most exciting possibilities is 3-dimensional glass components. Pre-fired glass with any dimensional characteristic will not be altered when fired with the PMC3 silver-clay. Similarly glass with an iridized or dichroic surface or a fired on decal will not fade during the final firing.

Another advantage that PMC3 offers is the ability to use a low cost 'pellet kiln'. This specially designed ceramic kiln uses sterno (type) pellets as the fuel for a no fuss firing procedure (see addendum 3 on page 84 for more details). This kiln cannot maintain annealing temperature to anneal glass and therefore it cannot be used to fire projects that contain glass (like the one we did here) but you can fabricate many designs, including projects with CZ's and achieve incredible success.

*Sheet Type Clay Enables The Jewelry Designer To Create Accessories That Feature Crisp Folds And Smooth Curves. (Note: Most Items In This Gallery Have Other Forms Of PMC Combined With The Paper Type).*

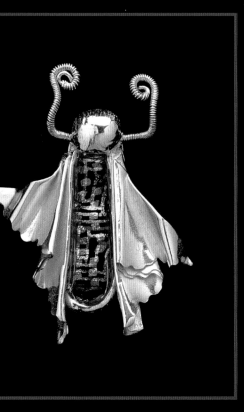

# FABRIC FOLD PENDANT
## Using The Fabric-Like Characteristics To Advantage

Sheet type clay feels like a thin sheet of vinyl. It can be folded and creased into crisp origami shapes (the Japanese art of folding squares of paper into representational shapes) or it can be pleated and gathered like soft fabric. Sheet type clay can be trimmed with patterned craft scissors or decorated with craft punches. Since the sheet does not contain water it does not dry out, greatly extending your working time.

I find it helpful to plan my design for the sheet type material using a piece of fabric or paper about the same size as the sheet clay (2-1/4" / 5.7 cm square). Use this sample to practice your technique of forming and to plan the design, cutting and shaping with the craft scissors, punches, folding and/or gluing until you have achieved the desired result.

## MATERIALS

**5 gram package PMC+ sheet, white glue, 16 gauge fine silver wire**

## EQUIPMENT

**Programmable kiln, ceramic fiber kiln shelf, paintbrush, stainless steel wire brush, burnisher, rotary tumbler, decorative craft scissors and paper punches**

## PROCEDURE

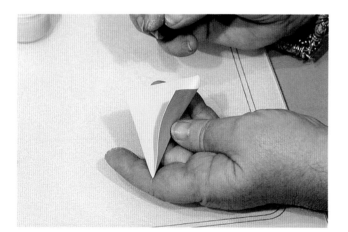

**1.** Designing for the sheet type clay may seem a bit peculiar at first. This is because it has a different textural feel that is somewhat like a sheet of vinyl or very thin leather. It is a good idea to find a piece of fabric or paper that has a similar texture and feel to the sheet clay and use it to explore new project design concepts prior to opening a package of the clay.

**2.** I have decided to make a free form pendant that I will decorate with loose beads and wire wrapping after firing. I want to have some wire loops sticking out on each side of my fired piece to facilitate the beads and wire wrapping so the first step is to cut a 2" (5 cm) piece of 16 gauge fine silver wire. Then use round-nose pliers to create the loops at both ends or create a spiral or other design on the wire ends (see examples in gallery photo on the previous page).

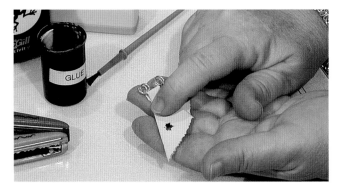

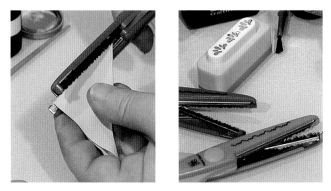

**3**. Remove the sheet clay from its package and fold it according to your design plan. Sheet type clay is very thin and I recommend using it double thick by folding it over itself or sandwich 2 layers together prior to your project fabrication.

**4**. An effective way to embellish the edges is to trim it with decorative craft scissors. Here I am decorating the leading edge of my brooch. The detail photo (right) shows the blade design on two of my craft scissors. They are available in a wide variety of blade patterns from scalloped to serrated.

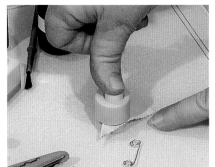

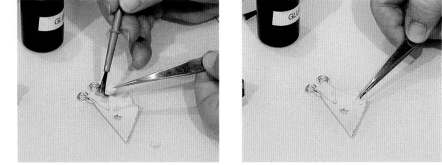

**5**. Another effective tool to use when working with sheet type clay is craft punches. Again you will find a large variety of designs available (this photo shows 4 different punches). I created the butterfly earrings, shown in the gallery photo on the previous page (top center), simply by 'punching' them out. The same butterfly punch was used for the necklace at lower left where I used both the punched cutout as well as the negative background to create a matched set.

**6**. I need to attach the wire to my piece by either folding the sheet over the wire, allowing the wire ends to extend beyond the sheet or attaching the wire to the back with a little paste clay. The punched out parts can be utilized as an interesting design element. Here I am placing the cutout leaf design on the pendant's surface. Remember to cut (or punch) a hole in the design to be used to mount the jump ring if the item is to be used for a necklace pendant.

**7**. When your sculpture design is complete, dry it in the normal way. Remember that the sheet type clay contains no water so it will not dry and harden.

**8**. Fire the pendant on the ceramic fiber kiln shelf as directed in addendum 1 on page 80. Smooth the surface of the fired piece with a stainless steel wire brush or polish it in a rotary tumbler with stainless steel shot (see page 86).

## OPTIONS AND OBSERVATIONS:

Don't be afraid to bend and twist this sheet type clay to add lavish folds or wild wrinkles. Sometimes a 'happy accident' turns out to be a superlative design. Just as with any other jewelry sculpture you could add CZ's (Cubic Zirconia), lump clay with texture, or create some decorative syringe extrusion.

Sheet type clay is very thin and I recommend using it double thick by folding it or putting 2 layers together. Make especially sure that you have double folds on the edges of the piece or you could reinforce the edge by placing a line of syringe clay on the underside or as a decorative element on the surface.

Sheet clay will not dry or become rigid the way the other forms of silver clay do. This extends the 'working' time but also means you may need to use a little white glue (standard crafters clue) to hold the folded sheets together while your fabricating your design. Try to use as little glue as possible and be sure to dry the glue completely with a hair dryer before firing.

This clay may feel different than the other clay types but it is completely compatible with all PMC+ clay types. Use them all in any combination that your artistic heart desires.

Don't waste any of the left over pieces or cutoffs. Place them into your paste jar and the sheet type clay will readily dissolve into paste type clay (you may need to add a bit of water).

# addendum 1

Firing your project is a very important step toward the successful completion of your jewelry piece. Firing will transform your sculpture from a lackluster lump of dried clay into a magnificent piece of sculpted fine silver. While it is possible to shape your piece after firing it is certainly much easier to make adjustments prior to firing. Take some time to refine and perfect your work now to save yourself time and disappointment later.

Precious Metal Jewelry Clay is nothing more than extremely small particles of precious metal, either .999 pure silver or 22K gold, suspended in a water based organic binder. During the firing process the binder burns away leaving a fully fused silver or gold piece. Shrinkage occurs as a result of the sintering process as the precious metal melts and fuses together, filling in the space that was originally occupied by the binder.

## The Importance of Drying

It is essential that all projects be thoroughly and completely dried before firing. If an item is fired before it is dry there is a great risk that it will crack or even break apart as the moisture tries to escape. You can air dry your sculpture (overnight is best) or dry it using a heat source such as a hair dryer, an electric heated serving tray, an electric griddle (or frying pan), a toaster oven or even a standard kitchen oven (set on lowest temperature). No matter which drying technique you utilize you must test to ensure your piece is completely dry. Place it on a shiny metal surface, such as a piece of aluminum foil or the inside of the lid from a candy tin. Leave the piece on the metal for several seconds and then remove it. Look on the metal for a 'ghost', which is actually a water vapor mark that is present if the piece is not completely dry. A second method is to hold the piece against your cheek (do this only when the piece is cool, don't pick it out of a hot electric griddle and immediately place it against your cheek). The skin on your face is particularly sensitive to temperature and if the piece is not completely dry, it will feel cool against your cheek. When you're sure your piece is completely dry, fire it according to the applicable table below.

## PMC+ Silver Clay Material

This material is available in lump form, syringe form, paste form, and sheet form. All forms can be used together in a single item and can be fired at the same time using the same firing schedule. The firing schedule gives you 3 choices for temperature and holding time. As you can see the lower temperature firing requires a longer holding time. If your piece is made up from PMC+ silver clay and contains only CZ's or other lab grown stones you can safely use the higher temperature and shorter hold time.

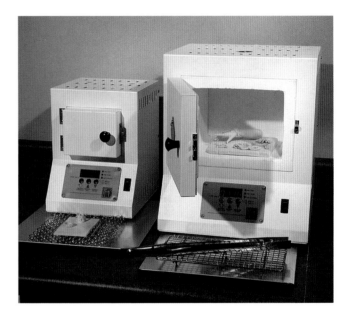

However if your piece contains glass components you should use the lower temperature with the longer hold time. You can fire one piece or several pieces at the same time. Just leave a reasonable space (at least 1/2" / 1.3 cm) between each piece on the kiln shelf.

Important Note: If any piece in the firing contains fused glass in any form you must use the firing schedule and procedure for PMC+ and glass (see page 81).

## The firing schedule for PMC+ is:

| Temperature | Hold Time |
| --- | --- |
| 1650°F / 900°C | 10 minutes |
| 1560°F / 850°C | 20 minutes |
| 1470°F / 800°C | 30 minutes |

## Special Instructions For PMC+ and Glass

Firing art glass and PMC+ at the same time requires a modification in the firing schedule. The temperature and hold time is different but more importantly the rate at which the kiln temperature increases from cold to the desired target temperature is also different. Glass is more susceptible to thermal shock and it is important to increase the temperature more slowly than with PMC+ alone. In addition an item that incorporates glass must be placed on a piece of shelf release paper to preserve the smooth finish on the back surface of the glass.

Sculptural clay and silver wire brooch enhanced with an amber stone set in a syringe bezel. *Photo by: Rob Stegmann*

The temperature ramp speed (increase in temperature) must be at a moderate rate of about 1500°F/ 816°C per hour. In other words it should take about 1 hour to reach the desired hold temperature of 1470°F / 800°C. Once that temperature has been reached you must hold it there for 30 minutes.

After the 30 minutes of hold time, the glass item must be 'crash cooled' by opening the kiln door to allow it to cool rapidly from 1470°F / 800°C to 950°F / 510°C. Open the door and watch the pyrometer as the kiln temperature decreases. When the temperature reaches about 850°F / 455°C close the kiln door. Retained heat in the kiln chamber and walls will cause the temperature to go back up after a few minutes. If the temperature goes above 1,000°F / 535°C, repeat the 'crash cool' process until the temperature remains below the 1,000°F / 535°C point. This crash cooling process will prevent devitrification (hazing or clouding) of the glass surface. Finally close the kiln door and leave it closed (do not even think about taking a peek) until the pendant has cooled slowly to room temperature (this will take several hours, it's best to simply leave it overnight).

## PMC3 Silver Clay Material

This product is the newest addition to the PMC family. Continuing from the development of PMC+, Mitsubishi has created another category of clay that takes advantage of even smaller metal particles than in PMC+. The positive effect this has is to reduce the firing temperature that allows a more varied use of glass and makes possible a different kind of kiln. Shrinkage is the same as with PMC+, about 12%.

### The firing schedule for PMC3 is:

| Temperature | Hold Time |
| --- | --- |
| 1290°F / 700°C | 10 minutes |
| 1110°F / 600°C | 45 minutes |

## PMC Standard Silver Clay Material

The main differences between the PMC standard clay and the other PMC silver products are the shrinkage factor and the firing time. PMC Standard shrinks about 30% whereas PMC+ and PMC3 both shrink about 12%. This is mainly due to the microscopic particle size. PMC standard particles are larger (than PMC+ & PMC3) and more binder is required, this means when the binder has burned off the size will naturally be smaller.

### The firing schedule for PMC Standard is:

| Temperature | Hold Time |
| --- | --- |
| 1650°F / 900°C | 2 hours |

Note: You can combine a firing of PMC Standard items with items made using either PMC+ or PMC3. This material can withstand the higher temperature and longer firing time with no adverse effect. However you cannot fire an item that contains glass or natural stones.

## PMC 22K Gold Clay

This product is manufactured using a mixture of 22K gold (91.7%) and pure silver (8.3%) particles and suspended in the same organic binder as the silver clay. The shrinkage factor for PMC Gold is about 14% (as compared to the wet clay size). PMC Gold can be fired together with PMC silver clays or separately prior to combining it with silver clay material.

### The firing schedule for PMC Gold is:

| Temperature | Hold Time |
| --- | --- |
| 1650°F / 900°C | 10 minutes |
| 1290°F / 700°C | 90 minutes |

Smaller PMC+ and PMC3 pieces can be fired quite easily using a butane torch. Pieces that have an overall even thickness work best with this method (e.g. a ring, a small pendant, an earring, etc). The advantage of the butane torch firing method is you can fire your piece in just a few minutes and you don't have to heat up a kiln to fire just one item.

Finish the clay piece as normal (sand, file and shape it) and be sure it is completely dry. This is always important but especially when using the torch firing method. Any moisture in the piece will quickly turn to steam when you apply the torch and as the steam expands rapidly it can cause the clay to crack, fragment and possibly fly apart.

## MATERIALS

Any small, evenly shaped item made from PMC+ or PMC3 material. Important Note: You cannot use this method on any item that contains glass, stones, silver wire, or any findings. These add-on's normally cannot withstand the high, rapid heat of the torch.

## EQUIPMENT

Butane torch, butane fuel, tweezers, heat-proof surface (e.g. cookie sheet), kiln shelf (or soldering block)

## PROCEDURE

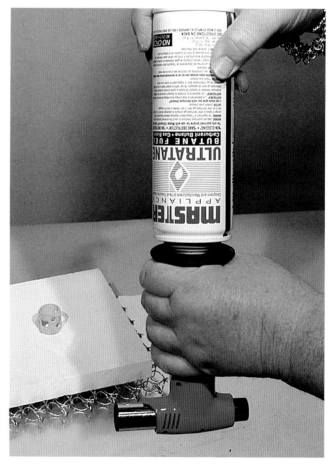

1. Finish your piece in the normal way. Be sure it is completely dry and finish the surface with fine sandpaper or a buffer block.

2. Work in a well-ventilated area. Place the kiln shelf (or soldering block) on the heat-proof surface and place the dried clay piece on the kiln shelf.

3. Fill the butane torch as directed by the manufacturer (as shown in the photo at right). Ignite the torch, following the manufacturer's directions. Adjust the fuel flow so that the inner blue flame is about 1-1/2" (4 cm) long. The outer flame should be about 3/4" (2 cm) longer. Aim the inner flame slightly above the piece you are firing.

**4.** Move the torch in circular motion keeping the flame continuously in motion across the entire piece. Use the outer flame at first to warm the piece then slowly move the flame closer to increase the intensity of the heat being applied. As the temperature increases the organic binder will begin to flame and then quickly burn off.

**5.** Continue to heat the piece using the circular motion until it reaches the 'sintering' temperature (sintering means: to cause to become a coherent mass by heating without melting). You have reached sintering temperature when the piece is faintly glowing with a visible orange color. As soon as the orange color appears begin the firing period of 2 to 5 minutes, depending upon the size of the piece. Be sure to use a timer to insure that the firing period has passed. It is difficult to judge the passage of time while working with the torch.

**6.** Be careful not to overheat the piece because you can actually melt it. If the surface turns from orange to a shimmering 'wet-looking' silver color, immediately move the torch farther away from the piece to reduce the heat. The shimmering look indicates the surface is starting to melt.

## OPTIONS AND OBSERVATIONS:

Use the butane torch to fire pieces made from the PMC+ or PMC3 silver clay material only.

Items that have CZ's (Cubic Zirconia) or casting grains can be fired with the torch firing.

Hollow forms should not be fired with the butane torch These must be fired in a kiln due to the smoke and fumes.

Complex pieces or items with varying thickness should be fired in a kiln. Complete sintering of the silver may not be possible due to difficulties with combustion and even heat distribution.

**7.** When you have completed the full firing cycle simply turn the torch off and let the piece cool down to room temperature. This will take a while so be patient or you could risk a serious burn. Once cooled finish the piece in the normal way.

PMC3 can be easily and economically fired in this ingenious kiln. The lower section is strategically shaped and the upper lid is lined with insulation fiber that enables the solid fuel pellet to bring the kiln interior up to the optimum firing temperature for the correct length of time to fire PMC3 clay material. Simply place the fuel pellet in the bottom of the kiln, place your PMC3 items on the metal screen shelf, put on the lid and light the fuel. In approximately 20 minutes the fuel will be burned and your silver clay item will be finished firing.

## MATERIALS

Pre-measured solid fuel pellet (similar to the fuel type used in a chafing dish) or gelled alcohol fuel, long match or butane stick lighter

## EQUIPMENT

PMC Hot Pot, Heat Proof Surface

## PROCEDURE

1. Place the bottom section of the kiln on a heat proof surface in a secure and ventilated location. Open (unwrap) the fuel pellet package and place the pellet in the bottom of the kiln. If using the gelled fuel, fill the fuel cup (not shown) with the fuel and place the cup in the bottom of the kiln.

2. Position the metal grill on the kiln and place your PMC3 project(s) on the grill screen.

3. Place the upper section of the kiln on top of the lower section and centered over the grill. Make sure the flame arrestor is in place on top of the kiln.

4. Ignite the fuel through the large hole on the side of the kiln, using a long wooden match or a butane fireplace stick lighter.

5. Allow the fuel to burn completely. This should take approximately 20 minutes. Then let the kiln cool for a while before removing the lid to retrieve your fired piece. There is no need to wait for the kiln to cool to room temperature, just use oven-proof mitts to remove the lid and the fired items inside.

6. Finish and polish your fired jewelry items in the standard manner.

### Safety:

Supervise the entire firing and make sure the kiln is sufficiently away from anything flammable. It may seem obvious but do not touch the ceramic kiln with your unprotected hands until it has cooled completely.

# BUTANE TORCH SOLDERING
## Modify & Attach Findings
### addendum 4

Sterling silver is an alloy (see alloy in the glossary on page 12) that contains 7.5% copper. This alloy adds much needed strength to pure silver especially valuable for use in fine gauge wires. Unfortunately the copper content produces a fire scale (a black tarnish) during firing and for this reason we do not recommend combining Sterling silver and silver clay in the fabrication of a piece.

However, there are times when Sterling silver is the best choice, especially when thinner, more delicate wire is required for items such as earring wires, earring studs, or prong mount findings (for natural stones). When you need the added strength of Sterling finding parts on your PMC piece simply solder them on using a small butane torch and silver solder.

## MATERIALS & EQUIPMENT

**Butane torch, butane fuel, tweezers, heat-proof surface (e.g. cookie sheet), soldering block (or kiln shelf material), silver-paste solder, small paintbrush, sterling silver finding, fired and finished jewelry piece**

## EQUIPMENT

**Butane torch, butane fuel, tweezers, heat-proof surface (e.g. cookie sheet), kiln shelf (or soldering block)**

## PROCEDURE

  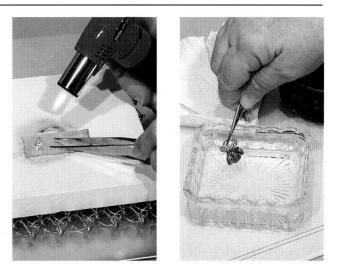

**1.** Be sure to work in a well-ventilated area. Fill the butane torch as directed by the manufacturer. Place the soldering block (kiln shelf) on the heat-proof surface.

**2.** Clean and finish your jewelry piece in the normal way but do not add a surface patina (see addendum 6, page 87) until after the finding has been soldered. The area where you intend to attach the finding must be very clean or the solder will not bond to it. Prepare the space by burnishing or sanding it slightly. Mix the paste-solder well. Use the tweezers to pick up the finding and use the paintbrush to apply a small amount of paste-solder to the back of the finding (that is side that will actually touch the silver jewelry piece).

**3.** Ignite the torch, following the manufacturer's directions. Adjust the fuel flow so that the inner blue flame is about 1" (2.5 cm) long. The outer flame should be about 3/4" (2 cm) longer.

**4.** Slowly warm the piece with the torch as if you were trying to dry the paste-solder. Continue to gently heat the piece, moving the flame in a very small circle motion, until you notice a slightly shiny area developing around the base edge of the finding that will appear to settle or melt onto the surface of the piece. Once you observe the melting immediately move the flame away from your piece and extinguish the torch. You must be very careful not to overheat your piece. It is all too easy to reach the melting temperature of silver and that will deform or destroy your jewelry sculpture.

**5.** Finally allow the piece to cool then clean the fire scale on the solder area by place it in a container of pickle solution to soak for a few minutes. Then remove and rinse in clear water. If desired the piece can be finished with an antique solution (see addendum 6, page 87). Or give it a high shine by polishing it in a rotary tumbler with stainless steel mixed shot (see addendum 5, page 86)

A fired silver clay jewelry piece will have a white-colored surface. This visual effect is a result of the rough surface texture that is easily polished using a stainless steel brush, a piece of fine steel wool or an extra fine emery cloth. Brushing produces a matt finish with an elegant and stylish look. Or you could mix a matt finish with selective bright spot finishing by using a burnishing tool. As a final touch you could add a patina (see addendum 6 – page 87) or you could finish it with a overall mirror bright polish.

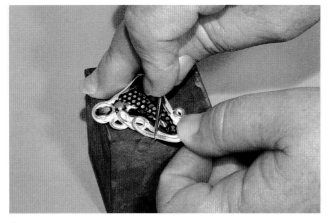

**1.** Burnishing your piece will give the surface a hand wrought look. You can burnish your piece selectively, leaving some areas untouched, or cover the entire surface with burnished strokes. Place it on a rubber block and press the burnishing tool firmly against the silver surface. Rub the tool back and forth across the silver surface, taking care not to scratch the surface with the point of the tool. It should not take long to bring up a beautiful shine, especially if you were careful to sand and finish your piece completely in the bone-dry clay state before firing.

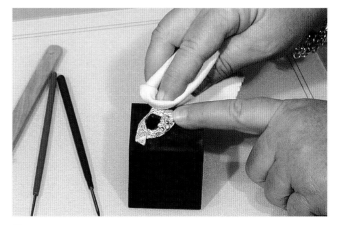

**2.** To achieve a super bright mirror finish you must do the final polishing using progressively finer abrasives and polishing materials. Begin with fine emery cloth, from 400 to 600 grit (or use the rotary tumbler to get to this point). Then move forward through the finer grades of emery cloth (1000, 1200, 1800 grit) using them with water to facilitate the sanding. Finish with a Jeweler's rouge cloth.

**3.** For an overall bright finish by far the easiest method is to use a rotary tumbler with stainless steel mixed shot. Simply use the stainless steel brush to remove the bulk of the white-colored surface then place your piece, or several pieces at the same time, in the tumbler. Add just enough burnishing fluid or 1 drop of dish soap along with water to cover the jewelry and the stainless steel shot. Turn it on and let it tumble away for 20 to 60 minutes or even longer. The longer you tumble the piece, the stronger (work hardened) and brighter it will become.

# PATINA SURFACE FINISHING
## Antique Look for Your Jewelry

# addendum 6

Some of the pieces illustrated in this book were finished with a surface patina. Simply dip a finished jewelry sculpture into a warm solution of liver of sulfur and the surface will take on an elegant, aged appearance.

The color range produced using this liver of sulfur patina process moves from a yellowish brown and progresses through gold, green, blue, purple and black. Sometimes you also get shades of red in combination with the other colors. These patina colors are not completely stable and may change over time. This is just the natural aging process that is common to all silver and is simply the result of ordinary tarnishing.

## MATERIALS

Liver of sulfur (solid crystal form), 2 insulated containers (e.g. coffee mugs), stainless steel tweezers or forceps, paper towels, finishing block, emery cloth, fired and finished jewelry sculpture. Optional items: an oven-proof ceramic pan (e.g. Corningware™) and a small hot plate (or use your stove top).

## PROCEDURE

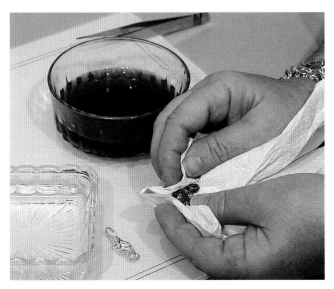

**1.** You will want to do this patina procedure in a well-ventilated area because the odor can be quite pungent (sulfur has a smell that is often compared to rotten eggs). Open the liver of sulfur container and take out a small chunk (pea size or equivalent) and dissolve it in 1/2 cup (120 ml) of hot (almost boiling) water, (for the photo we used a clear glass bowl, but it's best to use an insulated mug for this). If you are using a hotplate (stovetop), dissolve the liver of sulfur using the oven-proof ceramic pan and maintain the temperature at about 150°F / 65°C. Be careful you do not bring the solution to a boil. It is the heat and the length of time of the dip that will determine the subsequent color.

**2.** Have the other insulated container nearby that contains clean water (cool or lukewarm). Pick your jewelry piece up using the tweezers (or forceps) and plunge it into the hot solution. The silver piece could also be hot but it does not need to be. Heat will increase the patina reaction speed with which the silver reacts with the solution. If the solution or the jewelry piece is too hot, the reaction will be so rapid that you could lose control over the process.

**3.** If you cannot use a hot plate to keep the solution warm, make sure to use the solution as soon as you have dissolved the liver of sulfur in hot water in the insulated mug. In addition you could try heating the silver piece before dipping it into the solution (use your torch for this). This is a slower process because the cooler solution tends to diminish the patina's reaction. It is the combination of heat and the length of time of the dip that will determine the color of the final patina.

**4.** Quickly remove the piece and rinse it in the clean water. The clean water will stop the chemical reaction immediately. Take your piece out of the water to see if you have the desired patina color. If it is not dark enough or has not reached the color you would like (remember the color sequence described in the opening paragraph), you should continue the procedure of dipping and rinsing the piece until you have achieved the desired effect. Remember that this is not an exact science.

'Fossil Amulet' This neck pendant has a lizard skin texture. After the silver was fired the fossils were embedded using wire wrapping techniques. *Photo by: Rob Stegman*

## OPTIONS AND OBSERVATIONS:

To achieve the Ancient Clay look (see project 8, page 45), do not brush the piece before dipping it. For my 'Ancient Vessels' I only partially brush (polish) the surface, leaving some portions of the white-colored surface (unpolished). I then dip the piece at different angles and hold it only partially in the solution. The result is a variegated, crusty-shiny effect. The Vessels look like little ancient artifacts. In time they will become more even darkened if you do not seal the color with a jeweler's lacquer. I prefer to allow the pieces to age arbitrarily.

Black And Silver Finish. To acquire the elegant black and silver finish (see Calusa Mask page 37), polish the piece and then leave it in the liver of sulfur solution until it blackens completely. Rinse well with clean water and sand off the surface with 600 grit wet and dry emery paper. You can even use the emery paper under water to facilitate the process. Alternatively you could place your piece into a rotary tumbler with stainless steel mixed shot and burnishing liquid and tumble it for 30 to 60 minutes. The piece will be bright silver on the raised areas and black in the recessed areas. Complete the process by polishing it with a burnisher and/or a jeweler's rouge cloth.

There are other solutions available that you could use in place of the liver of sulfur. These alternate solutions produce different antiquing effects depending on their chemical make-up. No matter what solution you use be sure to follow the manufacturer's instructions for its use.

# ORGANIC CORE MATERIALS
## A Journey To The Center
### addendum 7

Core materials are used as a central form to fabricate a shape using the silver clay material (lump, paste, sheet or syringe type). The core form allows you to precisely shape the silver clay and retain that shape as the piece dries. Finally the core material must be capable of safely burning out during the firing process to leave a hollow central core in the silver jewelry sculpture.

Over the years we have tried many different materials in our classes to use as a core. A core material must be a non-toxic organic substance that will burn out completely and cleanly from your silver clay form. We have used such things as soda crackers, cheese puffs, noodles, bread (moistened with water and shaped), cereal, seeds, pine cones, leaves, twigs, nuts, paper, paper clay and cork clay. All of these materials work to some degree (some better than others) but we found that the most reliable and sculptural among these is cork clay.

Some materials are tempting to use as a core but may produce toxic fumes, heavy smoke or leave undesirable residues during firing. One such material is Styrofoam, which produces toxic fumes as it burns. I strongly recommend that you do not use synthetic materials for core forming. The fumes and possible fire hazards produced by these materials are real health concerns for people (or companion animals) and it can be difficult to ascertain which synthetic materials (if any) are safe to burn.

**1.** Cork clay (available from silver clay dealers and teachers) is easily modeled into any shape and makes an excellent internal structure for silver clay fabrication. Make your shape for a bead or any other sculpture design that you desire. Build your shape around an armature, such as a toothpick, that will allow you to hold the core as you apply the silver clay. In addition the hole left in the silver when the armature is removed will allow the smoke to escape during firing and will also allow you to remove the small amount of ash that will be left inside.

**2.** It is imperative that the cork clay form be completely dry before you start your fabrication. I prefer to dry mine by leaving it to set overnight. I find slow drying to the most reliable. Alternately you could dry it in a toaster oven set at 150°F / 65°C for a few hours or use your drying box (see page 20). If the cork is moist inside a finished silver clay piece when it is fired, the heat will turn the moisture into steam and the escaping stream will often develop enough pressure to damage or destroy your piece.

**3.** HAVE FUN! This clay medium and the hollow forming process will save hours of time (as compared to traditional jewelry hollow forming methods) and will provide numerous opportunities for you to produce unusual shapes.

## OPTIONS AND OBSERVATIONS:

Keep all unused portions of the cork clay tightly wrapped and in a zip-lock bag. Unfortunately dried out cork clay does not react well to being re-moistened. Store at room temperature. Mildew spots can develop on older cork clay but this will not affect the use of the clay and will burn off in the firing. However, if you have allergies to mold and mildew you might want to consider discarding the clay or at least the portion that has the mildew.

Do not add water to dehydrated cork clay. If you have two pieces of cork clay to join together, you could moisten the pieces in the area where they will join but usually a little pressure and the moisture already in the cork clay is sufficient to join the pieces.

Cork clay will smoke slightly as it burns so be sure to fire in a well-ventilated room (or even outside). If you notice smoke coming out of the kiln, DO NOT OPEN THE KILN DOOR! Doing so will only supply additional oxygen that could trigger a flash fire, endangering you or anyone standing in front of the kiln.

There will be a small amount of green ash residue inside your piece. This is easy to remove by cleaning the piece in running water after it has cooled.

# GEMSTONES
## Types & How To Use Them

Many man made or 'lab grown' gemstones can be safely fired in the kiln as part of a silver clay sculpture. If you are not certain that the gemstones you have will fire safely you should test them before you use them in one of your creations. To test a stone simply place it in the kiln while you are doing a standard firing of other pieces. If it holds its color and shape then you are 'good to go'.

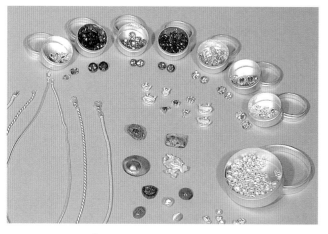

## Cubic Zirconia Gemstones

Cubic Zirconia is a man-made stone grown by a relatively fast method that involves extremely high temperatures applied inside a crucible containing Zirconia powder, a stabilizer and a Zirconia metal that oxidizes as it melts. The bottom line is Cubic Zirconia gemstones (CZ's for short) are downright stunning. Although the stone is often considered a cut-rate substitute for a diamond it is best regarded as an attractive stone in its own right. CZ's are eye-catching, available in a significant range of colors and they look first-class, so use and wear them with pleasure. I recommend using CZ's for your first stone experience because they are inexpensive, are very heat resistant (they can even be fired with a torch) and look impressive in any jewelry piece.

One note of caution: Not all CZ's are created equal. If you are not sure your CZ supplier has tested their stones for color and structural stability you will need to do this testing yourself before using a stone in one of your pieces. There is no need or excuse for disappointment.

## Laboratory Grown Gemstones

You can trust laboratory created synthetic stones to fire safely and will not change color, crack or melt. The chemical composition of these gemstones is nearly identical to the natural stones. They are made with a high temperature process that speeds the crystal formation process that takes nature hundreds of years. Most are perfect without inclusions and since they do not have inclusions the heat of the kiln firing does not normally fracture the stones. At the same time, you must be careful not to cause thermal shock by reducing the temperature of the piece too rapidly after firing. This can result in damaged stones.

## Be Wary of The 'Synthetic' Stone

Synthetic is a term that refers to any type of man made gemstone. This could be a duplicate of the chemical and physical properties of the natural stone or an imitation of the natural stone through the use of other materials, such as glass or even plastic. Therefore, you need to ask for laboratory grown stones.

Be cautious if you run across some laboratory grown gems called 'doublets'. They may be laboratory grown but they actually have two layers. The bottom layer is usually colored while the top layer is clear. The problem is that top clear layer may melt at higher temperatures. This 'problem' can be used for an interesting effect if you know it is going to happen. Two common examples of laboratory grown doublets are simulated emerald and peridot.

If you have a stone that you're unsure will stand up to the kiln firing you should test the stone at 1110°F / 600°C for 45 minutes in the kiln. If you know the stone is too soft or if it is too precious (or expensive) to risk, then plan on using a traditional setting where the stone can be attached after the firing. You can set a fine silver bezel wire into the silver clay and fire it in place (see project 14 – page 67). After firing, place the natural stone using traditional jeweler's techniques.

'Fancy Flower' made with hand formed lump clay, fine silver wire and a lab grown ruby crystal. *Photo by: Rob Stegman*

# How To Set The Stones

## Natural Stones

You can kiln fire some natural stones but you must only fire those stones that are at least a 7 or higher on the MOHS scale (a measure of the relative hardness of minerals). Stones such as, granite, quartz and the corundum family meet this benchmark. Other natural stones are too low on the MOHS scale to fire successfully e.g. bone, fossils, turquoise, and amber. A stone lower than a 7 will fracture and may even crumble in the kiln at temperatures of 1650°F / 900°C. Some stones that are 7 or higher may survive the heat OK but could have a color shift or may have small inclusions that could result in cracks later on.

**Method 1**- Setting Directly into the Clay (for heat resistant stones only)

CZ's and laboratory grown corundum gemstones can be fired with PMC. Cut a hole in the clay form you are working on to set the gem and allow light to pass through the stone. Make the hole slightly smaller than the diameter of the stone so the stone will not fall through the hole. Use tweezers to handle and place the stones. If the clay form you are working on is thicker than the height of the stone, you can press the stone into the clay until the surface of the clay is just above the widest part of the stone, known as the girdle. Make sure that there is clay below the stone so that the point of the stone is not exposed.

To set the stone with the syringe method, first cut the light hole and then encircle the hole with the syringe clay extrusion. The circle of syringe clay must be high enough to support the stone and capture the girdle of the stone. It usually takes several circles of the syringe. Gently place the stone into the clay circle and make sure that the table of the stone (the top) is level to the surface your jewelry piece.

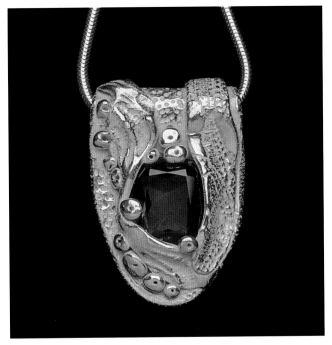

'Sculpted Simplicity' a slab-formed pendant (see project 1, page 21) using a lab grown amethyst. *Photo by: Rob Stegman*

A carved bone face looks out from a collar of fine silver feathers. *Photo by: Ken Devos*

**Method 2** - Setting with pre-made fine silver prong settings (any stone can be set using this method)

Commercially produced prong settings are available made of fine silver and calibrated to accept many typical size faceted stones. You can attach these settings directly to your jewelry piece before or after drying and include it in the firing. Since the material is fine silver (the same material as PMC) firing will not darken or weaken the setting (as will happen with a sterling silver setting).

Place the prong setting gently into the moist clay or use a small amount of syringe clay to attach the setting to your piece. Finish with a small amount of paste type clay on the inside bottom edge of the setting to ensure there are no open spaces. Fire the completed piece (including the prong setting) using the same kiln temperature and time determined by the other components of the piece. Since a fine silver setting is a softer material than sterling or gold settings I recommend that you tumble the piece after firing, using a rotary tumbler with stainless steel shot, for at least 1 hour. This will work harden the prong setting and make it stronger.

To set the stone, simply position it carefully in the setting cavity then gently push one of the prongs against the stone. Now move to the prong directly opposite and push it against the stone. Repeat the process with the other prongs until all have been set. Make sure that the prongs are firmly against the stone and that the stone does not move or rattle in the setting.

**Note:** You can use Sterling silver prong settings, which are stronger than fine silver, for stone setting. However Sterling silver should not be fired in the kiln. Instead Sterling silver prong settings should be soldered to your jewelry piece after it has been completed and fired. (See Addendum 4 – page 85 for more details)

# REPAIR, RECYCLE & REBUILD
## Everything Is Good

Jewelers have always been very careful to collect every minute particle of 'scrap' silver and gold to use in future projects or to sell back to the refiners for re-use. A very fortunate advantage to working with PMC is the ease with which it can be reconstituted. Those of us who work with this material all of the time have a 'never ending paste jar'. We place all of our crumbs, scraps, scrapings and unused clay pieces into the paste jar, add a small amount of water and stir for instant paste.

Just be sure to keep each clay type separate (i.e. PMC Std vs. PMC+ or PMC3). The paste is so wonderful for covering everything from leaves, pods and paper sculptures to butterflies. The more paste you have, the more things you learn to turn into silver. You begin to do with silver clay what Midas did with gold.

While working with the clay it may dry slightly and begin to crack. Simply use a water-dampened paintbrush to remoisten the clay and continue to form your design. It's best to apply the water in small amounts, and add more water as it is absorbed into the clay. Clay coils are notorious for drying out and it's always a good idea to moisten coils with water on a paintbrush before shaping.

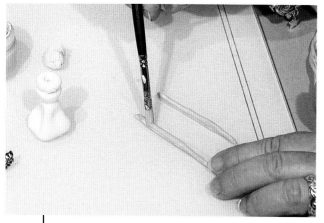

It is important to keep any unused portions of lump clay wrapped securely in plastic food wrap. Even clay that is wrapped will tend to dry out. When this happens simply infuse a small amount of water to the clay, place the moistened clay into a piece of plastic food wrap and knead it in your fingers. The plastic wrap will prevent the clay from adhering to your fingers and allow you to keep all of the clay in one package. Knead the clay well to mix the water throughout the clay.

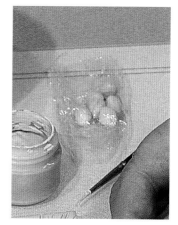

If the clay has become very dry or even if you have dried it to the bone-dry stage it can still be reconstituted (as long as you haven't fired it). Cut or break the clay into very small pieces and place them into a small, lidded container (a 35 mm film canister is perfect). Place just enough water into the container to cover the clay pieces but not so much that the clay becomes paste (unless that is what you want). Allow the clay to soak overnight. Once the clay has absorbed the water, place the clay lump into a piece of plastic food wrap and knead as described above. This final step is the real secret. It is important to insure that the clay has a uniform level of moisture throughout.

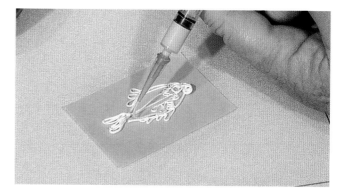

Even after you have fired a piece do not despair if you do not like the piece. I have a saying that there are no bad pieces, simply pieces which still need work. One of the wonderful things about PMC is that even after it has been fired you can add more clay to change the overall appearance and design. Simply add some syringe work (as I'm doing in the photo above), add some formed lump clay, Cubic Zirconia or whatever you like and fire the piece again.

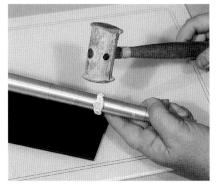 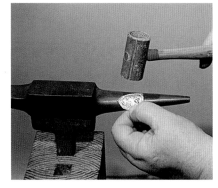 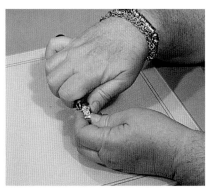

If your fired piece needs to be reshaped you can use a jeweler's rawhide mallet to gently re-shape a ring (see photo above) or add a curve to pendant (see photo above center) Note: do not curve a pendant that has CZ's or glass cabochon as you could loosen or damage them.

Another way to recycle finished-fired pieces that you're not happy with is to cut them into pieces and use the pieces as design elements to enhance other silver clay projects. You can refire these 'salvaged' silver pieces several times with no adverse effects.

Remember, the flexibility of this material allows you to work and rework the clay both before and after firing. There always is a way to reuse the clay before firing or to recycle the silver after firing to create exciting new silver pieces. Don't stop until you are pleased with your creations!

# SAFETY
## Remember to Work Safe

## addendum 10

- PMC has been certified to be safe and non-toxic. It conforms to ASTMD D4236 requirements, as indicated on the package insert.

- Practice sensible hand washing protocol before starting to work, while in the workshop, and especially when you have finished working.

- Do not eat in your work area, do not work in your eating area.

- Always pay attention to what you are doing, remember better safe than sorry!

- Handle sharp items carefully.

- Supervise children in the work area (or better yet keep them out of your work area).

- Watch the dog, cat, birds or any companion animals you have and keep them away from the work area. Did you know that you can kill your bird with fumes from burning polymer clay, Styrofoam or over-heated non-stick cookware?

- Kilns are hot during and after firing. Take care and use long tongs and/or gloves in placing and removing pieces from the kiln.

- Use heat-proof surfaces in front of the kiln and whenever using a torch. Keep a fire extinguisher handy at all times.

- Do not inhale dust from the kiln fiber blanket, kiln shelves or chemicals used in the studio.

- Wear eye protection when using power tools such as a flex shaft.

- Follow all manufacturers' safety guidelines for tools and chemicals.

# INDEX

# INDEX

## Sources

### PMC Clay Materials:

To find a convenient distributor for the clay materials, kilns and assorted tools featured in this book contact:

PMC Connection
Toll-free: 1-866-762-2529 (in USA)
Phone: (239) 463-8006
Fax: (239) 765-0680
Email: pmcconnection@aol.com
Website: www.pmcconnection.com

Orchid Brooch and Floral Ring - From the 3D stamp molding project starting on page 38. *Photo by: Randy Wardell*

# Wardell
## PUBLICATIONS INC

### Instruction, Inspiration and Innovation for the Art Glass Communnity

e-mail: info@wardellpublications.com   website: www.wardellpublications.com